The Motorless Flight Series

THE GREAT AMERICAN BALLOON BOOK:
An Introduction to Hot Air Ballooning

MANBIRDS: Hang Gliders & Hang Gliding

THE WILD, WONDERFUL WORLD
OF PARACHUTES AND PARACHUTING

In Preparation:

HALF MILE UP WITHOUT AN ENGINE:
The Essentials, the Excitement
of Sailplanes & Soaring

The Motorless Flight Series

THE GREAT AMERICAN BALLOON BOOK

An Introduction to Hot Air Ballooning

Bob Waligunda and
Larry Sheehan

Prentice-Hall, Inc., Englewood Cliffs, New Jersey 07632

The authors wish to express their appreciation for permission to reprint quotations from the following:

© 1962 American Heritage Publishing Company, Inc. Reprinted by permission from *The American Heritage History of Flight*

Hawthorn Properties (Elsevier-Dutton Publishing Co., Inc.) from the book, *Riders of the Wind* by Don Dwiggins © 1973 by Don Dwiggins.

Printed in the United States of America
Prentice-Hall International, Inc., London
Prentice-Hall of Australia, Pty. Ltd., Sydney
Prentice-Hall of Canada, Ltd., Toronto
Prentice-Hall of India Private Ltd., New Delhi
Prentice-Hall of Japan, Inc., Tokyo
Prentice-Hall of Southeast Asia Pt. Ltd., Singapore
Whitehall Books Limited, Wellington, New Zealand

10   9   8   7   6   5   4   3   2   1

Library of Congress Cataloging in Publication Data

Waligunda, Bob.
  The great American balloon book.
  (Motorless flight series)
  Includes index.
  1. Hot air balloons. 2. Balloons—Piloting.
I. Sheehan, Larry. II. Title. III. Series.
TL638.W34 629.132'522 81-2638
ISBN 0-13-363614-3   AACR2
ISBN 0-13-363606-2 {PBK.}

To Ed Yost, the pioneer, whose presence is
felt in every significant development
of modern hot air and gas ballooning

The authors would like to thank the following people for
their assistance and cooperation:

Jim Winker, Raven Industries, Inc.
Claudia Oakes, Smithsonian Institution
Bill Murtorff, Balloon Federation of America
Otis Imboden, The National Geographic Society

Contents

Foreword by Ben Abruzzo

Ever since *Double Eagle II* made the Atlantic crossing, the popular attitude has equated ballooning with high-risk adventures like mountain climbing or deep-sea diving. And certainly there is an element of danger in any attempt to set a new ballooning record. But most ballooning activities do not fall into this category and indeed involve very little risk. That is why I am so pleased to find that the emphasis in this new book is on the fun side of ballooning. Flying a balloon is such a unique delight that it would be unfortunate for people to think it is too dangerous or expensive to even consider getting involved in. In his book, Bob Waligunda has done a great job explaining how easy it really is to take up the sport—and how hard it is to give it up once you have started.

Bob has not neglected the more technical considerations in ballooning either. An experienced pilot and instructor himself (one whom I have flown with on numerous occasions), Bob has included the detailed training syllabus he uses in his own flight school. This will give readers an idea of the many subtleties involved in the art of flying a balloon. Bob makes the point that nothing can replace experience in grooming ballooning skills and I couldn't agree more. More so than any other form of flying, ballooning is an art and it takes time to develop the intuition or sixth sense to fly the balloon masterfully in all conditions.

Bob Waligunda was one of the first to convey the magical quality in ballooning to a wide public audience some years ago in a TV special that followed him on a cross-country trek from the Golden Gate in San Francisco to Central Park in New York City. Now with this new book on all aspects of the subject, he has created as fine an introduction to the sport as can be found. I hope you will enjoy reading it just as much as I did.

Welcome to ballooning!

Albuquerque, NM

Part One
THE BALLOONING
OF AMERICA

Chapter One

Introducing the Magical, Many-Sided World of Ballooning

Welcome to the magical, colorful, and sometimes wacky world of ballooning.

Imagine, if you will, that this book is a waist-high wicker vessel, sitting under a huge nylon canopy, brightly painted and filled with warm air. The craft is set in a green field under a clear blue sky, and there is a gentle wind in the trees.

The craft is ready to ascend. You are invited to climb on board. We want to take you on a flight through the unforgettably special, endlessly changing, and always surprising world of ballooning. Our flight may be on a slightly zigzag course—because the balloon, more than any other man-made airborne craft, is at the mercy of the winds' direction—but we know it will never get boring. And you'll never have to fasten your seat belts, either—balloons don't need to bother with such things.

Along the way, we will explain what is involved in learning to fly your

Whether you are looking up at balloons from ground level, or down at other balloons from inside one, the sight is awe-inspiring.

(Raven Industries, Inc.)

A nineteenth-century wedding in Central Park. Balloons and romance have always been intertwined. (National Air and Space Museum, Smithsonian Institution)

Every phase of modern hot air ballooning is fascinating to onlookers, from the stretching out of the yards and yards of fabric, to the deafening firing of the burners, to the moment when the envelope—nearly fully inflated—begins to rise from the ground like a great multi-colored beast. (Sky Promotions)

(Otis Imboden)

(Sky Promotions)

Aeronauts are treated like celebrities wherever they go. Sometimes the drivers of their chase vehicles are treated like stars too.

8 **The Ballooning of America**

own balloon, but our main purpose here is not solely instruction. Indeed, becoming a licensed balloon pilot, or aeronaut, is not a skill effectively acquired from any book. It takes many hours of individual guidance from a qualified teacher.

Our main purpose, rather than to teach, is to inform and entertain. The time is ripe for the trip we are proposing. Ballooning as we know it has been with us for nearly two hundred years, ever since two Frenchmen named Montgolfier discovered lighter-than-air flight by filling a twenty-foot-high paper envelope with smoke and causing it to rise. But today, and especially in America, ballooning is undergoing a great renaissance. Space-age technology has made it possible to build safe, efficient, and reasonably priced balloons. Ballooning takes people out of themselves, as they normally live and breathe in the ordinary world, yet at the same time creates an experience that amounts to an exaltation of the self. Adventurous Americans are turning to ballooning in increasing numbers, finding in the activity an escape from the mundane character of modern life, as well as an opportunity to express their individuality in a safe, unique, and gratifying manner.

The development of synthetic fabrics and modern fuel systems using propane made it possible for ballooning to enjoy a rebirth in the early 1960s. From a handful of aeronauts in that decade, the sport has grown to the point where there are now more than 3,000 men and women certified by the Federal Aviation Administration (FAA) as balloon pilots. The number of both pilots and balloons is currently increasing at a rate of nearly 25 percent a year.

But ballooning is an activity that is more than the sum of its participants. Let's look at its many different levels of appeal to appreciate why there is something nearly universal in its quality, and why it crops up in so many different ways in our culture and in our consciousness.

BALLOONING AS FANTASY

"It's a dream," said one avid balloonist about his favorite activity. "My dream, but anybody else can have a piece. It's a giant floating magic mushroom, an earth-star mushroom that grows on air and heat instead of cold and damp. When the sun has gone down and the last light touches it, it's an enormous Japanese lantern suspended above the invisible land."

Merely to see a balloon, let alone ride in one, is to enter the world of the fairy tale. Humankind's age-old fascination with the idea of flight partially explains why the balloon makes such an impact on our imagination. Somehow, even though flight per se is commonplace in the aviation/space age, we have not become immune to its appeal. Presently, Americans fly on commercial airplanes at the rate of 200 billion miles a year. When a plane goes by, most of us no longer bother lifting our eyes. When a balloon goes by, all of us do.

In any case, ever since the Montgolfier brothers launched their idea on the world in 1783, artists and writers have been drawn to the subject, and this in

Going up in a balloon is the ultimate thrill. Shown are former New Jersey State Senator Raymond Bateman and his family with coauthor Bob Waligunda about to launch. (Sky Promotions)

turn has whetted the appetite of the public for more information on ballooning. Throughout the nineteenth century there was a steady stream of dime novels, plays, and articles devoted to the adventures of real or imagined aeronauts. In 1835 Edgar Allen Poe gave us "The Unparalleled Adventure of One Hans Pfall," the story of a man who journeys to the moon in a balloon to escape his creditors. Though not one of Poe's best stories, "Hans Pfall" contains details about the preparation for the flight and about the conditions of the flight itself that ring true. Jules Verne was equally attentive to scientific detail in his 1873 novel, *Around the World in Eighty Days*, the story of Phileas T. Fogg's perambulations, which today we may know better from the film of the same name starring David Niven. Actually, Verne's first successful book, *Five Weeks in a Balloon*, published ten years earlier, had much more detailed ballooning sequences in it. He also once wrote a delightful short story about an aeronaut who discovers in midflight that the passenger in the basket with him is a homicidal maniac.

A sequence from Woody Allen's *Stardust Memories* made use of the colorful materials intrinsic to ballooning. (Raven Industries, Inc.)

The film medium is uniquely equipped to capture the magical nature of ballooning. One high-ranking scene in the cinematic memories of most of us surely is the attempted departure of Dorothy and her dog Toto from the world of Oz via a fabulous balloon. Woody Allen, one of today's most respected film-makers, incorporated balloons in *Stardust Memories*. Coauthor Bob Waligunda served as the technical director for the ballooning segment of that film. In the pivotal scene, three Raven Rally AX-6s with identical markings, piloted by three balloonists in identical flying Red Baron garb, which naturally included goggles and white scarves, appear over the horizon, float across a dazzled garden party, then drop in and join the festivities. The strict requirements of lighting for the film, combined with the need for precise wind and weather conditions to fly the balloons in the right direction and at the right speed, made this scene extremely difficult to shoot. In the fantasy business, though, it's not unusual to spend six weeks just to get two minutes' worth of the director's imagery.

One of the most affecting tales of ballooning was not about a balloon craft, but what used to be called a toy balloon, yet it captured the fantastical spirit of ballooning to perfection. *The Red Balloon* by Alfred Lamorisse is a short film about a Parisian boy named Pascal, who is befriended by a stray balloon on his way home from school one day. The story tells of the boy's difficulties in trying to protect the balloon from unfeeling parents, teachers, and schoolmates, who do not understand or appreciate the unusual friendship. Eventually, a gang of young toughs in Pascal's neighborhood destroy the balloon with rocks—whereupon all the balloons of Paris break loose from their moorings, fly to the scene of the atrocity, organize into a kind of air brigade on the spot, and carry Pascal aloft, freeing him from his loss.

The stirring finish of *The Red Balloon*, with its message of affirmation and rebirth, points up the spiritual dimension of the ballooning fantasy. Time and again balloonists will allude to this in their own ways, but always respectfully and quietly, for it is essentially a private experience not easily shared in words with strangers. "Being up above it all, you can see what it all means," one pilot explains. "It's almost a godlike condition, but at the same time it is quite humbling. No one ever makes a sneer from a balloon. There's a feeling of oneness, benign and mellow and loving."

"The feeling was one of being so enmeshed with it all that I wasn't alone in the gondola at all" is how another balloonist described it. "I'm so together with everything around me that I feel I can see the relationship of the land to animals, to man, to the sky and the sun. There is no loneliness or depression or fear."

Balloons can have a slightly evangelizing effect even on people who don't fly in them but merely catch a glimpse of them in the sky.

Comic strips, one of America's most original art forms, are a natural habitat for ballooning because the simple visual statement of the balloon is so appealing and the possibilities for plot development are so rich. *Little Orphan Annie* once rescued an impertinent young prince in a balloon and taught him a thing or two about democracy while aloft. *Dondi* ran a series of episodes about a balloon piloted by the kindly but somewhat inept Professor Hobie ("Great heavens, I left my altimeter on the ground!"). In *Peanuts*, Snoopy and his scatter-brained bird friend, Woodstock, have made several low-altitude but high-humor ascensions. *The Wizard of Id*, *Broom-Hilda*, and many other strips have also introduced ballooning characters, and still others have taken advantage of the balloon to get off one-liners. In *Blondie*, Mr. Dithers complains about his wife to Dagwood one day at the office. "Cora and I had a big fight last night," he says. "We were arguing about hot air balloons. She said she wants to go up in one. And I said she was one."

Political cartoonists also get a lot of mileage out of the balloon image, using it to depict such unpleasant phenomena as inflation and the rising cost of living.

BALLOONING AS COMMUNICATION

Advertising and promotion are more prosaic forms of the art of communication, but they too have found in the image and idea of the balloon in flight a powerful tool for reaching people. That is why we see balloons in the background in magazine ads for companies like Pentax, or balloons shaped like light bulbs—officially, "flight bulbs"—touring the country to introduce consumers to a new product from Westinghouse. That is why Anheuser-Busch had a fleet of balloons on which were printed, in perfect fidelity, the labels of their various brands of beer, a magnification of that product on the order of 7,500 times.

Interestingly enough, the commercial users of the balloon have probably contributed as much to artistry in the skies as have the private owners with their strikingly beautiful individual designs. It may simply be another aspect of the Pop Art syndrome, but when a Canada Dry or Early Times label or the Paine Webber logo is enlarged many times and sent floating across the cityscape at 1,000 feet, the overall effect is attractive. Though it is a kind of floating billboard, the balloon does not make the slightly vulgar impression that does its distant cousin found along our state highways. The magic of the balloon itself allows these particular ships of the sky to transcend their commercial role.

Naturally, commercial balloons are at their most effective when set aloft in densely populated areas, or when used at events attracting large crowds. On such occasions, the balloons fly over the crowds with their message, or sometimes are actually made more directly part of the spectacle. One year at the Super Bowl in New Orleans two balloons, personifying the teams contesting the game, were brought on the field at half time to entertain the fans. However, gusty winds made it impossible for the balloons to go through the mock battle that had been scripted for them. In fact, the one representing the Minnesota Vikings blew downfield out of control, narrowly missed going through the uppers for a field goal, and landed in the stands.

Because of the inherently unpredictable nature of balloon flight, trying to stage anything with a balloon in free flight is difficult. Tethered flight, in which the balloon is held captive to the ground by means of long lengths of rope, is the usual answer for commercial pilots setting up in congested areas such as shopping malls or fairgrounds. An added advantage of tethered flight is that the pilot can give many more rides to people, which are enjoyable even though the craft doesn't go much higher than 100–150 feet.

In recent years, candidates for public office have begun using balloons in their election campaigns. One might have thought politicians would not want to be associated with a thing containing so much hot air, but apparently this irony has escaped them. In truth, they have found the vehicles a great attention getter,

Balloons in advertising: an early gas balloon used to promote a store opening in San Francisco in 1887. Today's hot air balloons "billboard" products indoors or out, to get their commercial message across in a big way. Balloons can be custom-made in virtually any shape or size, which gives them great versatility as an advertising medium. (National Air and Space Museum, Smithsonian Institution)

Introducing the World of Ballooning 15

Ballooning also has a long and varied military history, from the earliest days as observation platforms to early training balloons and barrage balloons. Many of the latter were moored high over London during World War II with steel cables to foil enemy aircraft. Balloons were even used to carry explosives; the one pictured is one of thousands launched by the Japanese military, which hoped they would carry across the Pacific and detonate in the continental United States. (National Air and Space Museum, Smithsonian Institution)

and even presidential candidates have used them for campaign publicity. (The FAA does restrict all aircraft, including balloons, from operating in the vicinity of important public figures, for security reasons.)

Before the age of antiaircraft weaponry, balloons played a communications role in times of war. In 1794 a French captain successfully directed a battle with Austrian and Dutch troops from a balloon. Thaddeus Lowe, a giant of nineteenth-century ballooning, organized the first corps of balloonists for President Lincoln during the Civil War. The balloons were sent up to observe rebel troop activities and pass along the information by telegraph to the Blues, and did in fact provide valuable battlefield intelligence on several occasions. During Bismarck's siege of Paris in the Franco-Prussian War in 1870, over fifty balloons carried mail and sometimes paying passengers out of the city, mostly by night. One of those passengers got farther than he had bargained for—the wind carried him all the way to Norway.

At the height of the Cold War, in 1955, balloons were used to communicate the Western political point of view to people in the Iron Curtain countries by showering them with millions of anticommunist leaflets. The thirty-four-foot balloons were launched from West Germany, soaring to 25,000 feet and drifting with the prevailing easterly winds into eastern Europe. Each one carried 100,000 leaflets and a Rube Goldberg-style device made out of a bicycle wheel, alarm clock, and two razor blades. When the alarm clock went off, it caused two motor-powered razor blades to move slowly around the rim of the wheel, sever the cords that were holding the various packets of leaflets, and thus release the propaganda.

BALLOONING AS SPORT

It is as a sport, hobby, or recreational pastime that ballooning exists for most people. Numerous races and rallies held throughout the United States every year feature a number of fun-type events in which the competition is distinctly low-key. The balloonists who vie for the several prestigious national and international titles in the sport, or who take part in the burgeoning professional balloon-racing circuit, naturally take their flights seriously and do their most to outfly their rivals in each meet. There are dozens of experienced pilots who can handle their balloons with expertise, under many different flying conditions, and these men and women stand out from the rank-and-file flier who goes ballooning strictly for the fun of it. But no single sport balloonist ever emerges clearly as "Number 1"—and that is a nice feature in today's winning-is-the-only-thing world.

"I have to be serious in my insurance business," one expert balloonist once explained. "If I went into any sport as seriously as that, I wouldn't have any relief, would I? Ballooning for me is tranquillity, an aerial dream of Walter Mitty."

There are a variety of competitive formats that balloonists can fly in, but the most popular is called the Hare and Hounds. Modeled after the horseman's fox hunt, this event calls for a leading balloon (the hare) to take off five or ten minutes ahead of the rest of the balloons (the hounds) and to drift with the winds, changing altitude from time to time to put the hounds off the track. After a prescribed amount of time, the leading balloon lands. The hound that lands the closest is declared the winner. Skill is involved in emulating the flight pattern of the hare balloon, but a lot of luck is needed, too, and no one who finishes wide of the mark feels like a loser.

Most balloon rallies are social, an excuse to get together and ascend en masse, and only secondarily to achieve some goal agreed upon beforehand. For example, two dozen balloonists gather with their gear on the Connecticut shore-line and decide to try to cross Long Island Sound. They lift off. The wind shifts and, instead of driving them across the water, sends them cruising along the shoreline toward New York City, finally ending up in public parks, schoolyards, golf courses, beaches, parking lots, and in one case Victor Borge's front yard in Westchester. Everybody has a good time.

This fickle nature of ballooning automatically keeps competitiveness to a minimum. *Sports Illustrated* writer Coles Phinizy put it this way:

> A balloon pilot may be totally charged up with desire, ready to do or die for God, country and Yale, but he is still dependent on his balloon. That's the rub. There is no such thing as an inspired balloon. All hot-air balloons are fat, indolent clowns, bulging with indifference. They can be made to ascend and descend, but they never go anywhere on the level unless pushed by the wind. Balloons simply do not care. (*Sports Illustrated* magazine, March 5, 1973).

BALLOONING AS SEARCH

There has always been a strong scientific bent in ballooning circles, and with it the desire to find out new things and to test new ideas. The earliest balloonists concentrated on the search for the most effective balloon-flight system itself. Then, as flying techniques improved and the mode of travel became more or less established, scientists in other fields began to see ways ballooning could help them collect data. Thus, as early as the 1830s, an American named Charles Ferson Durant proposed using balloons to study the upper atmosphere. At about the same time, John Wise investigated balloons as a means for collecting weather data, his main interest at the time. Wise became enthralled with the balloons themselves, and he made building and flying them his life, accomplishing more than seven hundred successful flights over forty years. He never lost sight of the scientific role the balloon could play, however, and eventually gathered enough information from high-altitude flights to prove the existence of the west-to-east jet

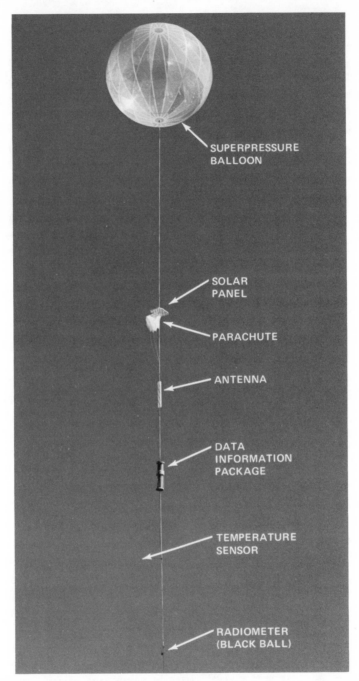

SUPERPRESSURE
BALLOON

SOLAR
PANEL

PARACHUTE

ANTENNA

DATA
INFORMATION
PACKAGE

TEMPERATURE
SENSOR

RADIOMETER
(BLACK BALL)

Balloons have long been employed in scientific research projects. Here, one hoists a radio signal reflector so ground-based transmitter and receiver sets can communicate. (National Center for Atmospheric Research)

stream over the American Continent. On the basis of that information, he became the first person to see the feasibility of a transatlantic balloon flight, and worked toward trying to do it himself.

Scientists in European countries also adopted the balloon as a research tool, sending them up equipped to take readings of atmospheric conditions. In the 1850s the first crude aerial photographs of the earth's surface were made from a balloon.

With the successful flight of the Wright brothers in 1903 and the subsequent mushrooming of the heavier-than-air aviation industry, the balloon's usefulness as a research tool was ignored, derogated, or just plain forgotten. But today the balloon is recognized once again for its ability to go places and do things no other craft can do, and once again it is allied with science in the search for truth. Government agencies and foundation-funded research teams have largely replaced the maverick and sometimes amateur scientists of old, and the projects they have launched are many times more complex.

Modern scientific ballooning started in the late 1940s when the Navy wanted to develop a new high atmospheric research tool. Using the new technology of the period, including plastic materials, it was possible to revolutionize the design of unmanned sounding balloons. This successful development led to what is known as the Sky Hook Balloon, which has since been used in tens of thousands of scientific research flights. These balloons typically have carried payloads, such as cosmic physics research experiments, weighing thousands of pounds at altitudes of approximately twenty-five miles.

Another type of project is the Equatorial Wind Experiment Program. Some 2,000 compact thirteen-foot-diameter Mylar balloons filled with helium and carrying sensitive data-collecting gear have been launched and for a three- to six-month period circle the globe at 48,000 feet, measuring wind velocity and air temperature and relaying this information to ground stations via satellite.

Another project called the Atmosat Program uses manned helium balloons to measure smog in our cities. The balloon can do this job much better than conventional aircraft because it does not generate wind, vibration, or engine exhaust, all of which distort instrument readings.

New Mexico scientists have launched a 28-million-cubic-foot balloon carrying 5,000 pounds of ultrasensitive instruments to an altitude of 112,000 feet, above our atmospheric shield. This $5 million NASA-funded program has already gathered data suggesting there is a stream of so-called antimatter coming from interstellar space, a finding that could have an important impact on theories about the origin of our universe.

A Princeton astronomer has sent a balloon to 80,000 feet with a telescope that will be able to study the stars without what is known as the "bad seeing"

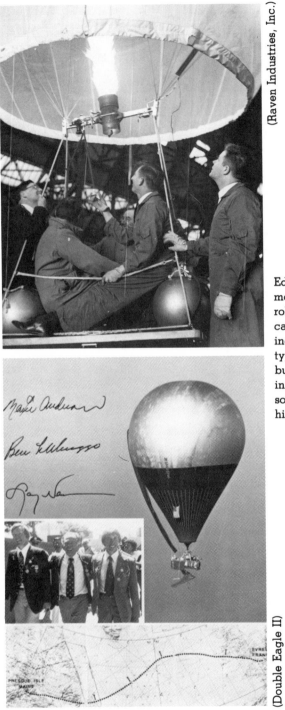

(Raven Industries, Inc.)

(Double Eagle II)

Ed Yost is regarded as the father of modern ballooning because of his role in developing a safe and practical hot air balloon. He is shown operating the propane burner on the prototype craft *Vulcoon* in 1960. Yost also built the gas balloon *Double Eagle II*, in which Ben Abruzzo, Maxie Anderson, and Larry Newman made their historic transatlantic flight in 1978.

caused by the earth's turbulent atmosphere. Balloons were also used in the observation of the comet Kohoutek in 1975.

Still more ambitious projects are in the offing. Scientists at the Franklin Institute in Philadelphia have proposed a solar-powered balloon station at the edge of space to serve as an observation and research platform. It would monitor weather on earth and relay information on the heavens, and could have an important defense role in surveillance and even combat-related missions. This particular balloon would be so big that at twilight, when the platform would remain sunlit for twenty minutes, to an observer directly underneath it on earth it would appear six times the size of our moon. Even Jules Verne would be impressed.

It is poetic justice of a kind that the development of the modern hot-air balloon, which created the resurgence in the sport today, was in fact the direct result of the scientific need to get at the truth of things. In this case, it was the U.S. Navy that wanted the facts. Specifically, the Office of Naval Research commissioned the firm of Raven Industries, Sioux Falls, South Dakota, to try to come up with a balloon that could be lifted with hot air and was reasonably easy to launch and operate. The balloons would be used for low-altitude research and would need to be manned. Raven had already built helium-filled polyethylene

Ed Yost and Don Piccard fly across the English Channel in 1963. The feat called attention to newly developed hot air balloon technology. (Raven Industries, Inc.)

balloons for unmanned data-gathering missions in the upper atmosphere. The Navy wasn't interested in that type of balloon because helium, like hydrogen, is an extremely expensive fuel, and gas balloons generally are cumbersome in preflighting and short on maneuverability during flight.

The Raven team that went to work on the project was led by a clever graduate of the Boeing School of Aeronautics named Paul E. (Ed) Yost. Yost married the idea of using nylon fabric for an envelope with the idea of using a burner rig fueled by propane and came up with a brilliant solution for the Navy's problem. When he tested the balloon himself, on October 22, 1960—lifting off near Bruning, Nebraska, and flying for thirty minutes—he ushered in a new age in ballooning. For although the Navy ended up shelving the project, Raven immediately saw the potential in marketing a recreational version of the military model.

Yost, incidentally, is the man who designed the ingenious leaflet-dropping contraption mentioned earlier. He holds more than twenty patents related to balloon-flight systems and personally holds six world records for helium balloon flight. In 1976 he designed and built the balloon *Silver Fox*, then took it on an extraordinary 107-hour-long Atlantic crossing attempt that ended near the Azores, seven hundred miles from the coast of Portugal. He also designed and built the balloon which did achieve the first crossing in 1978, with three other aeronauts aboard, the famous *Double Eagle II*.

BALLOONING AS ADVENTURE

The spirit of adventure underlies all the other aspects of ballooning we have mentioned. Almost all balloons are christened by their proud owners with names, and these names usually reflect adventurousness, too: *Glory, Jonathan Livingston Seagull, Roadrunner, Skywalker, Sky Schooner, Desert Dancer, Colorado High, Firebird, Rainbow, Sundance, Windsong, Fancy Free, Vision, Jolly Roger, Skybird, Odyssey, Island in the Sky, Freedom, American Free Spirit, America, American Dream, Emerald Star, Starship, Zodiac, Corona Borealis, Wild Wind*, and on and on.

"It has occurred to me, sometimes, late at night," confesses one balloonist, "when my head is not quite clear, when I've had too little sleep and too much champagne, that I don't want to fly a balloon at all. I want to *be* a balloon."

Two recent exploits more than any others brought world attention to the spirit of adventure in ballooning at its best.

In one exploit, three Albuquerque, New Mexico, businessmen named Ben Abruzzo, Maxie Anderson, and Larry Newman, became the first balloonists in history to cross the Atlantic Ocean. Their eleven-story balloon, dubbed *Double Eagle II* (in its predecessor, *Double Eagle*, Abruzzo and Anderson had failed in a previous attempt), made the trip from Presque Isle, Maine, to Miserey,

France, in five and a half days and nights filled with tense moments and numerous technical and personal challenges. Since 1873 at least fourteen unsuccessful attempts to cross the ocean had been made, some ending in tragic loss of life. One writer called their success, "a stirring reminder of the perils man faces in challenging nature, and the courage he displays in conquering it."

On their trip, Abruzzo, Anderson, and Newman covered 3,150 miles in 137 hours, six minutes, setting new world distance and duration records for gas balloons along the way. They received a hero's reception in France, similar in its emotional force to the one that greeted young Charles Lindbergh forty years earlier, when he conquered the Atlantic in the *Spirit of St. Louis.* Remarkably enough, the wheat field where *Double Eagle II* came down, on August 17, 1978, was only forty miles from Lindbergh's landing spot at Le Bourget airport northeast of Paris. And like Lindbergh, the trio answered the challenge voiced in these words of French author André Gide: "We cannot discover new oceans unless we have the courage to lose sight of the shore."

Little more than a year after *Double Eagle II* touched down safely, a much shorter but equally moving ballooning trip was planned and executed successfully. The flight lasted only twenty-eight minutes and covered only thirty-five miles, but news of it was received with warm and wild enthusiasm everywhere in the free world.

On September 16, 1979, Peter Strelzyk, a thirty-seven-year-old electrician with some earlier experience in the East German air force as an aircraft mechanic, piloted a homemade balloon with seven passengers aboard from Pössneck, East Germany, to a height of about 8,000 feet, over sentries, attack dogs, watchtowers, electric fences, land mines, and remotely triggered shrapnel guns mounted at leg, midsection, and head levels, down to safety and freedom in the town of Naila, West Germany.

Strelzyk and his wife Doris, age thirty-four, took along their two children, as did their good friends Gunter Wetzel, twenty-four, and his wife Petra, twenty-three. The four children, aged two to fifteen, crouched around containers of propane in the middle of the eighteen-square-foot flying platform, which had been welded out of scrap iron in Wetzel's basement. The four adults stood outboard on four iron rods, holding onto the lengths of nylon clothesline that held the platform to the balloon.

Their successful flight climaxed eighteen months of clandestine assembly and reassembly of the components needed for the flight. As far as knowledge of ballooning goes, they had to start from ground zero. They first devoured all the books they could find that were even remotely concerned with the subject. Then Strelzyk took responsibility for construction of the gondola and burner system, and Wetzel for sewing the giant envelope that would be required to lift them and their families out of a situation they later described as a "hermetically sealed workers' and farmers' republic (which) turns your children into opportunists and hypocrites."

Their ingenuity and persistence were incredible. The first envelope that Wetzel painstakingly created out of 8,000 square feet of cotton cloth—he told the store where he bought it that he needed it for tent lining for a camping club—failed to contain air when they attempted inflation. A second envelope was made out of a synthetic taffeta. To buy it in the large quantities needed without arousing suspicion, Wetzel drove a hundred miles to a department store in Leipzig and placed the order there—this time explaining that he needed it for making sails for a sailing club. This envelope did inflate properly, so a first flight was attempted, but it ended in failure when weather brought the craft down a scant two hundred yards from the border, and in the middle of the East German border patrol's "death strip," from which they all gingerly removed themselves.

Starting all over again, the men constructed a new eighty-two-foot high balloon. This time their flight carried them and their young families, with only the clothes on their backs, to the destination they craved. Actually they came down with such a thump in the woods near Naila that Wetzel broke his leg—the only casualty of the daring escape.

When Strelzyk and Wetzel were assured by the two amazed Bavarian policemen who came upon them that they were in fact inside West Germany, Strelzyk called for the families to come out of hiding in the trees, and also to bring the bottle of champagne they had taken on the trip. "We can open it now!" he declared joyously. "That's what the books say all balloonists do when they land!"

The flights of both the sophisticated helium-filled *Double Eagle II* and the makeshift hot air balloon of the audacious East Germans are surely this century's most glowing tributes to the spirit of adventure and freedom inherent in ballooning. There is a pilot's prayer, believed to have originated in Ireland, frequently seen on posters in ballooning circles. Chances are it was uttered instinctively by the world for the intrepid participants in both those flights:

> *May the wind welcome you with softness,*
> *May the sun bless you with his warm hands,*
> *May you fly so high and so well*
> *God joins you in laughter.*
> *And may He set you gently back again*
> *Into the loving arms of mother earth.*

Chapter Two

Gas Versus Hot Air: 1783 and All That

Perhaps the best way to explain the fundamental differences between the hot air-filled balloon such as was used in the East Germany escape flight and the gas-filled balloon used on the Atlantic crossing is to return briefly to France and to that remarkable year for aviation, 1783.

Working simultaneously and increasingly in the public eye as proof of the capacity for man to fly became more tangible, were Jacques-Étienne and Joseph-Michel Montgolfier, paper manufacturers doing business in Annonay, near Lyons in central France, and Professor J. A. C. Charles, a physicist who happened to be exploring the lifting properties of hydrogen at the time, under the auspices of the Academy of Sciences, in Paris.

The Montgolfiers were essentially engaged in some research and development at their paper factory. Having observed how bits of paper flew up the chimney when there was a roaring fire in the hearth, they experimented with filling a small silk bag with smoke. When they saw this creation float magically to

The first manned balloon ascension, November 21, 1783, made by the Montgolfier brothers. (National Air and Space Museum, Smithsonian Institution)

the ceiling, they determined to explore the possibility of manufacturing larger balloons. They started testing various papers to see which type might make the best fabric for a balloon. They were convinced that smoke, rather than the heat produced by fire, was what provided lifting power in their tests, and called this mystery agent phlogiston, a term derived from a Greek adjective for "burnt, set on fire."

The brothers' first success came on or about June 5, 1783, when they filled a thirty-three-foot linen balloon open at the base, or throat, from a smoky fire built from damp straw, with some old leather shoes thrown in for good measure. The balloon rose to a height of 6,000 feet and stayed aloft for ten minutes, floating across Annonay village for a distance of one and a half miles.

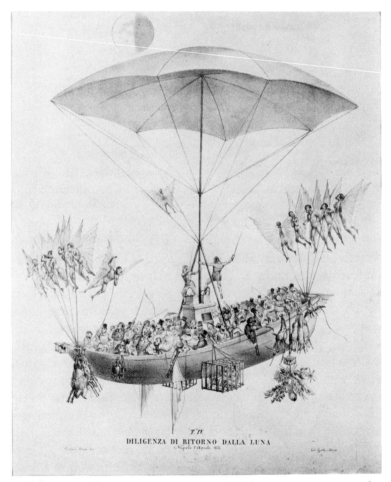

DILIGENZA DI RITORNO DALLA LUNA

A fantastical flying machine typical of the nineteenth-century aeronautical imagination. (National Air and Space Museum, Smithsonian Institution)

A modern gas balloon rises above a few of its hot air brethren. Note: The gas balloon is closed at the throat. (Ed Yost)

Next, and more or less on royal command, they traveled to Versailles and launched another, larger balloon, this one in front of Louis XVI and his court. It is probably impossible for modern audiences, hep to all kinds of moon shots and space probes, to imagine the state of mind of the onlookers as the Montgolfiers stoked their foul-smoking fire. It took them about ten minutes to generate the phlogiston needed to launch the balloon and the cage that had been attached to it, containing a rooster, a duck, and a sheep. This time the craft quickly rose to 1,500 feet, stayed up eight minutes and came down two miles away, with only the rooster, who had been kicked by the sheep, slightly the worse for wear.

The culmination of these hot air balloon trials came in Paris on November 21, 1783. J. F. Pilâtre de Rozier, who had successfully made a tethered ascension a month earlier, and the Marquis d'Arlandes made man's first aerial voyage. Present were the King and Queen and virtually the rest of Paris. (One writer has estimated that the crowd of 400,000 may have been the largest gathering of people in the history of the world to that time.) Lifting off from in front of the King in the Bois de Boulogne in a seventy-foot linen balloon decorated with zodiac

Needlepoint on this antique European chair depicts frightened peasants "slaying" a downed balloon. Such incidents actually occurred in the early days of ballooning. (National Air and Space Museum, Smithsonian Institution)

signs and the French royal symbol of the fleur-de-lis, the two men floated across the City of Light at approximately 3,000 feet, and came down safely twenty-five minutes later, five miles away on the other side of the Seine.

Meanwhile, physicist Charles had not been inactive. He had found that by pouring sulfuric acid over iron filings, he could produce hydrogen. He called it "flammable air," but in any case he knew that filling a bag with it gave him a balloon with considerable lift. He successfully launched his first gas-filled balloon, unmanned, in August. Then on December 1, 1783—only ten days after man's first hot air balloon flight—Charles and one passenger went up from the Tuileries gardens in Paris in a wicker gondola with a silk envelope filled with hydrogen, and drifted for two hours and twenty-seven miles in man's first gas-filled balloon flight.

It should be noted in passing that ballooning may have existed in ancient cultures. An interesting experiment was conducted in 1975 near Nazca, Peru, under the auspices of the International Explorers Society. In Nazca, on terrain once occupied by pre-Inca Indians is a complex set of markings, at first thought to be some sort of irrigation system, construction of which could only have been directed from some elevated vantage point. The purpose of the experiment was to see if a balloon made of fabric equivalent to ancient Peruvian materials and inflated with smoke from a fire pit in a manner likely to have been within the capability and style of the natives of the region 1,000 or 2,000 years ago, could fly.

Most cultures have myths and legends about gods, priests, and heroes who were able to fly. Peru is no exception, and some of the stronger stories concern a boy, Antarqui, who would fly above an enemy army and then report their movements back to his own people. Another refers to a bearded god who gave the Incas knowledge and when finished went to the shores of the Pacific and flew away into the sun.

More startling, and based on fact, not myth, is the evidence presented by a Jesuit missionary, Bartolomeu de Gusmão, who actually observed balloon flight in the depths of the South American wilds. He was recalled to Portugal to explain his findings, and in 1709 demonstrated a model hot air balloon to the king. This information has been generally available to modern researchers, but has also been generally ignored, possibly being considered fanciful. However, recent research into the original manuscripts held in Portuguese archives leave little doubt that Gusmão actually knew the principles of hot air flight and probably demonstrated it. The fact that his mission territory included northwestern regions of South America lends immense weight to the possibility that balloon flight was known and practiced there for centuries before being lost with some now extinct civilization.

The 1975 experiment resulted in a successful manned balloon flight lasting three minutes to an altitude of about four hundred feet. "It doesn't prove that the ancient Peruvians had the intellect or the innovativeness necessary to build a balloon," says Jim Winker of Raven Industries, which assisted in the project. "It does leave one with the feeling of plausibility that these people could very well have been the first balloonists. There may be other explanations for the Nazca markings, but this is certainly the best one I have heard."

After the events of 1783, balloon fever gripped all of France, and quickly spread to neighboring countries, especially Great Britain. (It didn't really get rolling in America until the 1830s.) A certain madcap atmosphere took over as new balloonists and their frequently fantastical craft took to the skies. People at launch sites sometimes tried to force their way into gondolas in their rage to fly. All manner of new products and customs appeared in the early nineteenth cen-

An artist's rendering of the gala day in Paris when Napoleon III's son was baptized. Over 300 balloons and parachutes were launched above the city for the occasion. (National Air and Space Museum, Smithsonian Institution)

tury that were cast in the image of the balloon. Women of society began to *dress* like balloons, as bell sleeves and hoop skirts came into vogue.

Increasingly elaborate and decorative balloons were built. An Italian count went up in one shaped like a boat. Others added oars or wings to their baskets. Stunts became positively rococo. Pilots lifted off the ground mounted on stallions, resembling equestrian statues called to heaven. Giantism eventually became the fad. In Paris a two-hundred-foot-high balloon was built to carry what amounted to a small six-room house. In its first (and last) flight it covered four-hundred miles before gale winds forced it down in Germany and dragged the "house" along the ground for ten miles, knocking senseless the elegantly dressed passengers inside.

Even the miscues and outright disasters of ballooning sometimes seemed more amusing than macabre. It was all so new and different. Balloons bounced into trees, fell into lakes, knocked chimneys off housetops. Passengers accidentally stunned earthlings with jettisoned sandbags or fell out of baskets themselves.

Poster luring spectators to an exhibition by an English balloonist. Such spectacles, which later spread to the United States, usually featured an ascent by a smoke balloon and a descent by parachute. (National Air and Space Museum, Smithsonian Institution)

Early on, particularly, many people were genuinely fearful of balloons. A band of French peasants laid into a downed balloon with pitchforks, then hitched the envelope to a team of horses and rode it around in circles until they were quite sure the monster was dead.

Within just a few years of the first flights, the activity that Marie Antoinette had called "the sport of the gods," relied exclusively on hydrogen (or, after 1903, helium) as the lifting agent. Then what had become of the first hot air balloons launched to such awe and excitement?

The montgolfiers (as hot air balloons are sometimes called today, in honor of their inventor) quickly proved to be too cumbersome and dangerous, at least if they were to provide anything like the kind of in-flight time that could be gotten with the charlières (as the gas balloons are often called, in honor of *their* inventor).

The problem with the montgolfiers was that regular application of heat was needed to keep the open-throated envelope buoyant, and this meant carrying a lot of weight in the form of straw to burn.

It also meant dealing with the hazard of controlling a fire aloft. This hazard was demonstrated clearly in a flight that ended in tragedy in 1785.

Pilâtre de Rozier, the daring fellow who had piloted the first manned hot air balloon, this time ascended in an experimental double balloon, one hot air and one gas, of his own design. About thirty minutes into the flight, either the open fire serving the hot air balloon got out of control and spread to the hydrogen balloon, or lightning or static electricity ignited the gas and set the entire craft ablaze. Pilâtre and his one passenger had no chance to escape alive.

As for the charlière type of balloon, its fuel was highly flammable, but no fire needed to be maintained on board, so that danger was reduced. And though it was very expensive to produce hydrogen, the fuel was easier to control and could be conserved. Since it was contained in a closed envelope, unlike the open-throated montgolfier type, the balloon could be piloted so that it stayed aloft much longer.

For all these reasons, the charlière or gas balloon became the balloon of choice for some 175 years. Not until 1960, when Yost succeeded in flying *Vulcoon*, his propane-fired prototype, over the Sioux Falls countryside, was a safe and sound hot air balloon option restored to the world.

The only exception of note to this trend was the use of smoke-fired balloons for exhibition purposes at the turn of the century. Aerial stuntmen wearing parachutes would go aloft in balloons that had been filled with hot air from smoky fires built in trenches, rise as high as 2,000 feet or until the air in the balloon began to cool, then cut themselves loose from the balloon and use parachutes to get back to ground level safely. Such "smoke ballooning" exploits provided the climax for many a state and county fair throughout the country.

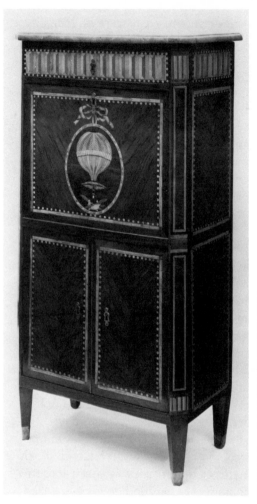

The balloon motif flourished in the decorative arts and fashions in the second half of the nineteenth-century. (National Air and Space Museum, Smithsonian Institution)

Don Piccard, a one-time associate of Ed Yost at Raven and later head of his own balloon-manufacturing firm, once expressed the qualitative differences between gas and hot air ballooning nicely. Piccard, incidentally, comes from a family of balloonists—his uncle, Auguste, and his father, Jean, twins, are both credited with inventing the bathyscaphe (an underwater balloon) for probing the ocean depths. His parents took a balloon to over 57,000 feet in 1934, the pilot in command being his mother, Jeannette, who thereby became the first women to enter the realm of space. His charlière-montgolfier comparison goes as follows:

> The serenity and detachment of the *gas balloon* is without question the ultimate sensation of voyage. In the traditional gas balloon you pay quite well for these rewards. One must have a great deal of technical training just to handle the first erection of the machine. *This normally takes several hours of sturdy* manual labor. The gas to inflate the balloon need not be extremely expensive, but realizing it will all be gone with the wind by the day's end makes it hurt a bit as it flows into the balloon—but then it also tends to cause one to prudently husband the use of it in navigating the balloon. This then is one of the criteria of a good pilot, that he can make economical use of his gas valve. It also insures that you don't get just a partial flight—you use what you have invested in time and money to best advantage so that each flight in a charlière becomes a real and worthwhile voyage.
>
> The life and action of the *hot-air balloon* makes it quite a different machine. The speed and lack of effort required to erect our everyday hot air sport balloon tends to give one a careless attitude as to prolonging the flight. One can joy ride this craft without worrying about conserving fuel; extravagant maneuvers are not really imprudent, but the name of the game. Kissing through the grain fields, bounding up through the tops of the trees and then down again into the next field to flirt with the flowers, this is the freedom of the montgolfier. While each exercise with a gas balloon is perforce a grand occasion well planned and executed to the finest degree, the hot air balloon becomes almost within the reach of everyday imagination.

The longest a hot air balloon has stayed in the air is twenty-four hours, eight minutes, and the farthest it has gone in one trip is 351 miles. Obviously, then, hot air balloons are not suited for really extended jaunts such as Atlantic crossings. But carefully prepared and well-piloted gas balloon flights such as that of the *Double Eagle II* can last many days and cover thousands of miles, as we have seen.

But economics are the bottom-line reason gas ballooning will remain out of the reach for most of us, and why this book is concerned primarily with the sport of hot air ballooning. The typical hot air balloonist would never refuse the chance, if it were offered during his or her flying career, to experience a gas-balloon flight. But with the cost of hydrogen for a typical flight running over $1,000, and the cost of helium now close to $3,000, clearly he or she, assuming an average bankroll, will opt for a comparable hot air balloon flight costing no more than $20 for propane fuel.

As we shall see, that's quite a ride for the money.

Chapter Three

The Ballooning of America

In this section we would simply like to take you on a quick tour of ballooning in the United States over the past two centuries, not only to supplement the bit of historical information already supplied, but to make you better aware of the rich and diverse tradition that ballooning really possesses in our country and the important role it has consistently played in our development as the leading aeronautics nation, and, finally, here and there along the way, to point out some of the odd little amusing or sometimes sad happenings that have always been part of the activity.

1783

The Ben Franklin Report Benjamin Franklin was in Paris as America's minister to France when the ballooning excitement began, but was not impressed at first, because "these machines must always be subject to be driven by the winds." But he soon saw the possibilities for the future and later mentioned some of them in a letter to a friend.

Convincing sovereigns of the folly of wars may perhaps be one effect of it, since it will be impracticable for the most potent of them to guard his dominions. Five thousand balloons, capable of raising two men each, could not cost more than five ships of the line; and where is the prince who could afford so to cover his country with troops for its defence as that ten thousand men descending from the clouds might not in many places do an infinite deal óf mischief before a force could be brought together to repel them?

He also foretold the role balloons would indeed play in future conflicts, "such as elevating an engineer to take a view of an enemy's army, works, etc., conveying intelligence into or out of a besieged town, giving signals to distant places, or the like."

1784

First Man up in Free Balloon The first American to ascend in a free balloon was Boston-born Harvard graduate, Dr. John Jeffries. He had become a Tory during the Revolution and was practicing medicine in London when his interest in ballooning was piqued by the exploits of French aeronaut Jean-Pierre Blanchard. Jeffries went up with Blanchard and several scientific instruments on November 30 before an audience that included the Prince of Wales.

First Tethered Flight The first reported American to go up in a balloon in America was thirteen-year-old Edward Warren. He rode a tethered thirty-foot hot air balloon above an enthusiastic crowd in Baltimore on June 23. The multicolored silk balloon had been built by Baltimore attorney Peter Carnes, who for reasons having to do either with his weight or his courage, so they say, was relieved to have such a daring young volunteer on hand.

A month later, Carnes did attempt a free flight from a Philadelphia jail yard, but he was thrown out when the balloon hit a building, and was lying on the ground in a daze while the crowd cheered his empty craft up and out of sight.

Not Banned in Boston The first article on aeronautics was published in America in the January issue of *Boston Magazine* (which also ran the text of General Washington's resignation from the army). The article was called "Explanation of an Air Balloon," ran two pages, and was illustrated by a picture of an aerostat outfitted with oars and rudder.

1785

Balloon Bites Dust in Connecticut The first balloon shot out of the sky in America was the creation of one Josiah Meigs of New Haven, Connecticut. Meigs made the mistake of launching his unmanned balloon near the village green just when the local militia was out on drill. The soldiers promptly brought the balloon down with accurate musketfire.

Boston Doctor Flies English Channel The first American to fly the English Channel was also Dr. Jeffries. He had been so pleased with his first experience aboard a balloon that he offered to pay all expenses if aeronaut Blanchard would let him go along on the Frenchman's planned attempt to cross the Channel.

According to Jeffries, Blanchard was unwilling to share the record-making flight with anyone, once going so far as to wear a weighted girdle to convince people that the balloon would be unable to lift two men successfully.

Finally, on January 7, the weather and the dispute cleared up and the American and Frenchman left Dover and made the first crossing, landing in the forest of Guînes, twelve miles inside France. They were presented to Louis XVI at Versailles, then fêted for two months by the French before Jeffries returned to London exhausted. He spent the last thirty years of his life practicing medicine back in Boston and wrote the first book by an American on ballooning.

The Tom Jefferson Report Thomas Jefferson was in Paris as Franklin's replacement at the time of the Blanchard-Jeffries Channel crossing, and wrote of his impressions on ballooning to Francis Hopkinson in the United States. He felt that:

> This discovery seems to threaten the prostration of fortified works unless they can be closed from above, the destruction of fleets and what not. The French may now run over their laces, wines, etc. to England duty free. The whole system of British statutes made on the supposition of goods being brought into some port must be revised. Inland countries may become maritime states unless you choose rather to call them aerial ones as their commerce is in the future to be carried on through that element.

Hopkinson's reply to this letter was in a lighter vein:

> We have not taken the affair of the Balloons in hand. A high-flying politician is I think not unlike a balloon—he is full of inflammability, he is driven along by every current of wind—and those who suffer themselves to be carried up by them run the risk that the bubble might burst and let them fall from the height to which the principle of levity had raised them.

1793

Man and Dog Make First Ascent The first free balloon flight on American soil wasn't to be for almost ten years after little Edward Warren's tethered ride, and it took off from the same Philadelphia prison yard used in the Carnes attempt. At the controls was that ubiquitous Frenchman Blanchard, who

The first manned balloon flight in America was made by French aeronaut Jean-Pierre Blanchard in 1793. (Penn Mutual Insurance Company)

was in the United States to escape the turmoil of revolution in his own country as well as to introduce balloon flying to the Yankees.

One of his patrons was President George Washington, who joined a crowd of 50,000 spectators, in what was then the nation's capital, to see man fly. Unfortunately for Blanchard, few of these thousands felt the need to pay for the two- and five-dollar tickets, when they could see the flight for nothing from almost anywhere.

Shortly after 10 A.M. on January 9, Blanchard and a friend's small dog and six small bottles of wine were launched and proceeded to cross the Delaware, while a mile up in the atmosphere. Forty-six minutes later, he landed in the New Jersey field of some armed and very suspicious farmers, who understood neither the balloon nor the language spoken by Blanchard and might have expressed their hostility physically if not for a "passport" signed by Washington, asking that whoever found the aeronaut to treat him with respect.

A local paper the next day reported that the ascent "was truly awful and interesting, and the slow movement of the band added solemnity to the scene."

Animals Overboard The first parachute drop from a balloon in this country was made on June 6 in Philadelphia—by a cat, a dog, and a squirrel, all attached to the same chute.

This stunt of Monsieur Blanchard was popular enough but not so lucrative as to become a standard in the financially frustrated Frenchman's repertoire.

1799

Federal Balloon Invented The first patent for a balloon in America was issued to one Moses McFarland on October 28, but all that survives in the way of information about the aeronautical device Moses had concocted is its name—"Federal Balloon."

1819

French Exhibitionists Ply Trade Ballooning regained public attention in America after becoming something of a lost art in the wake of Blanchard's flight, with the arrival of two exhibition balloonists from France, Louis-Charles Guille and a fellow named Michel. Ascensions were made all along the eastern seaboard and as far west as Cincinnati.

In a planned joint demonstration in Philadelphia on September 8, Michel had trouble inflating his balloon, and an impatient crowd rioted, destroying his balloon and all his gear and stealing his money.

In a solo flight in Jersey City on November 20, Guille flew to five hundred feet, then came down in his own parachute, thus becoming the first man to parachute from a balloon in America.

1825

First Female Up The first American woman to fly in a free balloon was one Madame Johnson. She ascended from Castle Garden in New York on October 20, in the balloon of French aeronaut Eugene Robertson. She was described by the New York *Evening Post* as being about thirty-five years old, wearing white satin and waving flags as they were launched. Together, they sailed across the East River and Brooklyn, landing in a marsh after being in the air for little more than one hour.

While aloft, Robertson conducted several experiments, including examining the effects of drinking champagne at high altitudes. He found this to be "peculiarly lively and stimulating."

Robertson's father was a famous aeronaut of Europe, having made more than fifty flights, and his brother Dimitri was the first to ascend from India in 1835. Eugene was also the first to balloon from Cuba, in 1828, and was flying from Vera Cruz, Mexico, in 1836 where he died of yellow fever. Before this, however, he had made another contribution to American aeronautics in training Charles Ferson Durant, who was to make the first flight in the United States by an American-born aeronaut.

A Fish That Flies The first patent ever issued in the United States for an aeronautical invention, whose plans survive on record, went to another Frenchman staying in this country so as not to lose his head in the political turmoil at home.

Edmond Charles Genêt had designed what looked like an enormous fish with moving tail, which would hold over a million cubic feet of hydrogen gas. Suspended beneath this was a platform on which were two horses supplying the power by driving a revolving wheel.

This craft never got off the ground, and though his patent was signed by President John Quincy Adams himself, Genêt received much ridicule. Today, however, the outlandish craft is recognized as being aeronautically sound.

1830

Preflight Poems a Hit Eventually hailed by Paris and London papers as "America's First Aeronaut," Charles F. Durant ascended from the site of his mentor's success, New York's Castle Garden, on September 9 in a balloon which he had constructed at his home. While aloft, he released two carrier pigeons indicating his position, and when he landed in Perth Amboy, New Jersey, thirty miles away and an hour later, he was hailed a hero and borne through the streets in triumph by enthusiastic citizens.

Durant's twelve flights during the next four years were always well-attended, for their own merit and because before each ascension, he would recite a humorous poem he had made up telling of the fantastic things he would see on this and other planets.

Durant foresaw many future uses for the balloon, such as predicting weather, delivering mail, and use in wartime. He also designed the first instrument just for aeronautics, a barometer for altitude reading which was immune to the hard knocks of balloon landings.

1833

First Ascension for Chief Black Hawk The first demonstration of ballooning to native Indians was made by Charles F. Durant at Castle Garden in June, before crowds estimated at 100,000. Led by the great Sac chief, Black Hawk, the group of Indians watched from a steamboat on which they had sailed from Philadelphia. The Indians were naturally impressed when the ascension went as planned, and Black Hawk later wrote (in his dictated autobiography) of the occasion, "We watched with anxiety to see if it could be true; and to our utter astonishment, saw him ascend in the air until our eyes could no longer perceive him." A newspaper report the next day alleged that the chief had also wondered aloud if the aeronaut might visit the Great Spirit while aloft.

1835

First Air Mail, Part One The first airmail to be delivered by a balloon in America, though not to its addressee, was carried aloft by Richard Clayton, a Cincinnati watchmaker whose passion for ballooning had been acquired in his native England. This young man first broke into the headlines in April of 1835 when he achieved a nine-and-a-half hour flight that took him some 350 miles (from Cincinnati to Munroe County, Virginia), at that time by far the longest aerial voyage recorded in America.

On the strength of his new fame, Clayton ascended on July 4 with a mail bag of newspapers and letters destined for the Atlantic coast. Due to difficulties maintaining his altitude, he only traveled a hundred miles, not even enough to get him out of Ohio. Upon landing he arranged for the letters and newspapers he had on board to be postmarked at a nearby post office, thus making it official mail even though after the fact.

1839

Professor Wise As a result of a balloon bursting on him during a flight this year, John Wise, the nineteenth century's foremost aeronaut, devised one of the most important safety features in ballooning—the rip panel. In this incident, Wise noted that the burst fabric flared out and acted like a parachute, permitting the disabled craft to float safely to the ground. (The maximum rate of descent of a balloon or a parachute is only 1,200 feet per minute.) Wise then considered the possible role some sort of controlled opening in the side of an envelope could play. He soon realized that a venting system, by dumping the hydrogen gas quickly, could greatly reduce the danger during landings. Previously, and especially in high winds, balloons upon landing could be dragged great distances over rocks and against trees. The pilot could prevent damage and injury if he managed to catch one of his grappling irons on something solid, but that wasn't always easy. The rip panel made such landings much more manageable.

Wise made over five hundred balloon flights from 1835 to 1879, when he disappeared on a flight over a stormy Lake Michigan at the age of seventy-one. In addition to developing the rip panel, he also discovered that muslin could be used as effectively as the traditional silk in the manufacture of envelopes, thus making ballooning more economical. His writings and lectures influenced many future aeronauts and also educated the general public about flight.

The record-setting feats of "the Professor," as he was called, became so well known that children's textbooks of the time carried such arithmetic problems as this:

"If Professor Wise can ascend in his balloon 4 times in 1 week, how many times can he ascend in 3 weeks? Why?"

1842

Idea for Dirigible Shot Down The first dirigible proposed in the United States was the brainchild of John Pennington of Baltimore. He wrote to Congress describing plans for his 234-foot steam-powered machine, which resembled a cross between a football and a katydid, and argued for its usefulness in wartime. The government rejected his application for development funds.

1843

Aeronaut Faces Congress, Gets Nowhere John Wise became the first aeronaut to raise the serious possibility of a transatlantic balloon flight by appealing to Congress for $15,000 to finance his mounting such a launch. Wise, who had a consuming interest in all aspects of science and particularly astronomy and meteorology, had proved to himself on several of his own high-altitude flights that the prevailing winds in the atmosphere were westerly and could be used to carry a properly built and piloted balloon to Europe from America.

On this occasion and two others, Congress listened to the Professor's ideas with deaf ears, and indeed found them a bit ridiculous.

An artist's sketch of the foremost American ballonist of the nineteenth-century, Prof. John Wise, floating over Washington, D.C. In 1843, he made an impassioned plea to Congress to fund an Atlantic crossing attempt, but was not taken seriously. (National Air and Space Museum, Smithsonian Institution)

1844

Edgar Allen Poe On April 13, the New York *Sun* scored a reporting coup by being the only paper to announce the first crossing of the Atlantic by a balloon. However, it turned out to be a hoax. According to the report, eight men led by Monck Mason, Irish writer, musician, and aeronaut, had made the crossing in three days and landed safely at Sullivan's Island in South Carolina.

As it happened, true ballooning exploits had captured the vivid imagination of Edgar Allen Poe, and his need for money led to his writing a fascinating journal à la Monck (who was indeed a balloonist). According to the journal, Monck's balloon set out for Paris on April 6 and "an unforeseen accident occurred" when the steering mechanism broke. They were driven toward the Atlantic by an eastern wind, and they decided to "take advantage of the strong gale which bore [them] on, and in place of beating back to Paris, make an attempt to reach the coast of North America." Monck was ever confident that they would make it safely across "this small pond" and felt that "the difficulty has been strangely exaggerated and misapprehended."

The hoax was as convincing as Orson Welles' Martian invasion show by the Mercury Theater on radio a century later.

The success of the story, as Poe later wrote, "was something beyond even the prodigious, and, in fact, if (as some assert) the *Victoria* did not absolutely accomplish the voyage recorded, it would be difficult to assign a reason why it should not have!"

1846

Mother Hubbard to Moon A version of the nursery rhyme "Mother Hubbard" was published in New York, and included this well-known verse account of the lead character and her dog:

> *They got in the car*
> *Of the Vauxhall Balloon*
> *But for want of more ballast*
> *Went up to the moon.*
>
> *Where the man with his sticks*
> *Kindly welcomed them in,*
> *To a seat, to a cake,*
> *And a quartern of gin . . .*

(Vauxhall was a reference to the *Royal Vauxhall*, a balloon that left England on a famous flight on November 7, 1836, and landed in Germany the next day. One of those on board was Monck Mason—the aeronaut who figured in Poe's hoax.)

1847

More Dirigible Ideas In 1847, Rufus Porter flew a six-foot model of a dirigible powered by a spring-loaded propeller around the Merchants' Exchange building auditorium in New York City.

This feat in Porter's life had been preceded by an impressive list of inventions, including a corn sheller, steam carriage, washing machine, and a revolving rifle that Samuel Colt bought for $100. Porter also cofounded the magazine

Scientific American in 1845 and featured his steam-driven *Aeroport* in one of the first issues.

He then formed a company to raise funds to build an airship capable of carrying three hundred passengers to California and its gold fields. This venture, like so many involving air machines, was doomed by lack of foresight and finances, but a hundred years later, Navy dirigible commander H. V. Wiley expressed surprise at finding "how many of the things incorporated in a modern airship had been forecast by Mr. Porter."

1856

Heigh-Ho Silver On July 4, before a crowd estimated as high as 50,000 people in Manchester, New Hampshire, French aeronaut Eugène Godard made an ascension on top of a horse for the first equestrian balloon ride in America. He subsequently repeated his act in numerous cities.

By this time showmanship of this sort had become increasingly important to balloonists, since it was often the only way to attract a lot of attention—and paying crowds.

1858

Should Have Let Go One of the more bizarre accidents in ballooning history occurred in August of this year. Ira J. Thurston, an experienced balloonist, and a friend had landed after a successful flight in Adrian, Michigan, and were releasing the gas. To hurry things along, Thurston removed the basket and climbed onto the top of the balloon. Unfortunately, there was still a considerable amount of gas in the bag and the bottom became closed off by dangling cord.

Instantly, the balloon swelled up again, rolling upside down as it went. Before he could think to jump off, Thurston was shot into the air, hanging down from what had been the top of the balloon. His body was not found until a month later.

1859

The Professor's Big Trip On July 2, John Wise set forth from St. Louis on probably the most famous balloon voyage of his long career. The *Atlantic* was an enormous balloon—the Professor hoped it would eventually carry him across the ocean of the same name—measuring 130 feet high, and sixty feet wide, with a 50,000 cubic foot capacity.

Passengers on the flight were fellow aeronaut John La Mountain, reporter John Hyde, and a wealthy balloon enthusiast by the name of O. A. Gager, who was paying for it all.

Professor Wise made a historic 800-mile flight in 1859 in his 130-foot high *Atlantic*. (National Air and Space Museum, Smithsonian Institution)

They ran into a storm over Lake Erie, which forced them to throw everything overboard, including the champagne intended for celebration, and cut off the lifeboat that they had strung to the gondola in case of a water landing. For over a hundred miles they raced along, sometimes skimming the turbulent waters, before reaching land and then crashing through the forest "like a maddened elephant through a jungle."

They came down in Henderson, New York, eight hundred miles from St. Louis. A bespectacled old lady was on the landing scene and remarked that she was "really astonished to see such sensible looking men in such an outlandish vehicle."

Air Mail, Part Two On August 16, John Wise received from the postmaster of Lafayette, Indiana, a mail bag containing 123 letters and twenty-three pamphlets for delivery in New York City, and took off with it in his balloon, *Jupiter*. Foul weather forced the craft down a few miles away, in Crawfordsville, Indiana. Wise returned the mail to postal authorities for forwarding to its proper destination. Though he had not taken mail as far as Clayton had in 1835, Wise nevertheless became the first to carry official air mail by balloon in America, because his payload had been postmarked prior to launch.

Samuel Archer King The first drag rope was used on a balloon flight in America on September 1, when Samuel Archer King copied an idea that had originated some years earlier in England and that helped gas balloonists control their flight altitude without constant elimination of ballast or gas.

The drag rope was simply a long, heavy rope attached to the gondola and allowed to hang free during flight. If the pilot wanted to check a sudden descent, he put out rope until it dragged along the ground, effectively reducing the total weight of his balloon and stopping the fall. If the pilot wanted to keep his ascending rate slow, he pulled the rope free of the ground, thus adding weight to the balloon and counteracting the rising air currents.

King was the most famous American aeronaut of the late nineteenth century and made over 450 successful ascensions in his lifetime.

John La Mountain A few months after his exciting trip across Lake Erie with Professor Wise, John La Mountain met newspaper editor John Haddock, and they decided to go for a short fly. Haddock said later that he expected "not to be absent from home more than ten or twelve hours at the longest, and to have a good time."

They left at 5:30 on September 22, rose rapidly to two or three miles height, and were soon breezing along in the darkness at over a hundred miles an hour. At nine o'clock, they landed in the middle of a Canadian forest. For the next four days they hiked through the cold in their street clothes and with little to eat. They finally came on the log cabin of "a noble-hearted Scotchman, named

T. S. C. Lowe organized a balloon corps for President Lincoln during the Civil War. The gas balloons were used primarily for observation and played a significant role in some of the action. The sketch of Rebel positions in Virginia near the Maryland border was made from Lowe's balloon on December 8, 1861. (National Air and Space Museum, Smithsonian Institution)

Angus Cameron" who told them they were 150 miles north of Ottawa. After a rest, they returned to Watertown, New York, which had thoughtfully put out a $1,000 reward for finding them alive, $500 if dead.

1860

T. S. C. Lowe On September 8 in Philadelphia, Thaddeus Sobieski Constantine Lowe of Jefferson, New Hampshire, another of nineteenth century America's most distinguished aeronauts, began inflation of the balloon he expected to carry him across the Atlantic. Practically twice the size of his great rival aeronaut's *Atlantic*, the *Great Western* was 200 feet high and 104 feet wide, and had a capacity of 725,000 cubic feet. It was so big that in the previous year, at the original inflation site at the corner of Fifth Avenue and 42nd Street in Manhattan, it drained the resources of the New York Gas Company, and the inflation had to be called off.

This time, in Philadelphia, it was the balloon that caused the problem. It burst.

First Aerial Photos The first aerial photographs of America were taken when drop-rope innovator King took a photographer by the name of William Black on board a flight over Boston. Black snapped several panoramas of the city.

1861

Jail On April 19, T. S. C. Lowe left Cincinnati in a second transatlantic balloon, somewhat smaller than his *Great Western*, on a test flight to the coast. After an uneventful ten-hour cruise, he descended in the northern reaches of South Carolina and was promptly surrounded by a hostile crowd. When some of the local planters mentioned the possibility of lynching him, Lowe showed his Colt revolver. That saved his neck, perhaps, but did not prevent the aeronaut from spending a night in a nearby jail as a suspected Yankee spy.

War clouds obviously were forming in the sky for balloonists as for everyone else.

First Aircraft Carrier On August 3, the U.S.S. *Fanny* became the country's first aircraft carrier when John La Mountain arranged to use it as a base for aerial reconnaissance from his balloon along the Potomac. La Mountain's effort had great psychological value for the inhabitants of Washington as his reports from on high effectively quashed recurring rumors of Confederate forces closing in on the city.

Abe: All Is Well As the Civil War began in earnest, T. S. C. Lowe became the first American to fire a telegram off to the White House from a balloon, and in consequence was named chief aeronaut of the Army of the Potomac.

On June 18 in Washington, Lowe ascended with two telegraph operators to demonstrate the feasibility of using balloons to observe enemy movements and communicate intelligence to the ground. The first airborne telegram was received by President Lincoln, who shortly gave Lowe the go-ahead to form the first American military balloon corps.

On several occasions during the next two years, Lowe and other aeronauts whom he recruited did indeed provide aerial surveillance from their balloons, which aided the Union cause. In time, however, the new unit became bogged down in administrative problems. Lowe quit the job in exasperation in 1863, and the corps itself quietly folded shortly after.

1863

Dr. Solomon Andrews On September 4, Dr. Solomon Andrews of Perth Amboy, New Jersey, successfully flew his airship *Aereon,* a project he had been working on intermittently for some forty years. As a youngster he had approached Durant for help on his brainchild, then later Clayton and still later Wise, but none of the noted balloonists were able to help him. The ship consisted of three eighty-foot-long cigar-shaped balloons held parallel to each other and supporting a basket underneath. For an admiring crowd of spectators and newsmen, Andrews piloted the huge craft in a spiral pattern at what one paper reported as a rate of 120 miles per hour.

Andrews was a multitalented individual—physician, mayor of his home city for three terms, and inventor extraordinaire. He held over twenty patents for, in addition to his airship designs, such items as the wickless oil burner and the country's first combination lock.

1873

Washington H. Donaldson On May 17, Washington H. Donaldson made the first successful flight in a balloon made entirely of paper, and got ten miles in it.

Such stunts were typical of the Philadelphia-born Donaldson and made him one of the most popular aeronauts of his day. In the post-Civil War era there was a considerable resurgence of interest in ballooning for its entertainment value, and ascensions were always being made in connection with holidays, circuses, fairs, and other public events.

Donaldson often worked for Barnum's Traveling Hippodrome. He was the epitome of the professional balloon exhibitionist of this time. A natural athlete and an inveterate entertainer, he was a daredevil in the air and loved to perform dazzling acrobatic or swinging rope feats while flying. His shows and his numerous scrapes with danger were always reported in admiring detail by the press—which he carefully cultivated by giving many free rides. While aloft during one show near the Atlantic Ocean, he jettisoned his basket and remained with the envelope alone, hanging by a rope. An unexpected wind swept him toward the ocean, and he was saved only when another dangling rope caught among the branches of the very last tree between him and the open sea.

Donaldson was not so fortunate in a subsequent flight two years later from Chicago. On July 15, 1875, he and a local reporter were brought down in a raging storm in Lake Michigan and drowned.

First Transatlantic Try The first attempt to cross the Atlantic by balloon was made on October 6 in the *Daily Graphic,* a 600,000-cubic-footer capable of carrying up to 7,000 pounds. The project, financed by the New York *Daily Illustrated Graphic* as a publicity stunt, had originally been the idea of John Wise. The Professor pulled out of the flight after a disagreement with the sponsors. That left his young assistant, Washington H. Donaldson, as pilot. Donaldson lifted off from a vacant lot in Brooklyn with two newspaper reporters on board. Four hours later they came down in a storm in East Canaan, Connecticut.

1878

Idea for Round Trip Works The first American patent for a machine that could carry a man through the air and then return to its starting place was granted to Charles F. Ritchel of Corry, Pennsylvania.

It looked like a bicycle suspended beneath a twenty-five-foot cylinder and could also be raised and lowered by rotating a propeller.

Ritchel gave several demonstrations of his invention in Hartford, Connecticut, where it was operated by a ninety-six-pound boy named Quinlan. He rode it over the Connecticut River and back again.

Ritchel's plans to reach the North Pole in this machine came to naught.

1885

Jump Specialist Captain Thomas Scott Baldwin made his first of hundreds of daring parachute jumps from a balloon at Golden Gate Park in San Francisco.

In a sitting position on a small seat below his balloon, he first ascended to 1,000 feet altitude. Then he pulled the rip panel in the balloon to commence the fall and create momentum to fill his chute. Finally he jumped, landed, and collected $1,000 from the park manager—one dollar per foot jumped, as agreed upon beforehand.

1887

New High Alfred E. Moore took along a professor, a photographer, and a newspaper reporter on a flight equipped with meteorological instruments to investigate high-altitude conditions. The balloon rose to 16,000 feet, breaking all United States records to date and causing the aeronaut to faint.

1898

Whose Side Is It On? The first American balloon to be shot down in wartime was sailing over the American troops in Santiago, Cuba, on July 1, advising them of the movements of the Spaniards, who finally deflated it with gunfire.

With the exception of its pilot, Colonel George Derby, the American troops were relieved: hovering over them, the balloon had drawn too much Spanish fire for comfort.

1903

Wright Brothers Start New Era On December 12 at Kitty Hawk, North Carolina, the Wright brothers made the first sustained and controlled flight in a powered, heavier-than-air craft, ushering in the aviation age as we know it today, and greatly reducing interest and experimentation in balloon flight for nearly fifty years.

1906

First Gordon Bennett New York *Herald* publisher James Gordon Bennett organized the first annual James Gordon Bennett International Balloon Race, an event for gas balloonists with winning based on distance as measured in a straight line from takeoff to finish, and not time flown. In the inaugural event, launched from Paris, American pilot Lt. Frank P. Lahm took first place, achieving a distance of 404 miles and finishing in Whitby, Yorkshire, England.

1912

Gas Balloonist Says Nyet H. E. Honeywell, an American entry in the Gordon Bennett race, landed in Russia on his flight and was clapped into jail by the Czar's secret police.

1914-1918

World War I The dirigible came into its own during WW I. Dirigibles were used for scouting by England, France, and Germany from the beginning, but by January 1915, Germany had equipped them with bombs and made a first raid in England, killing two people. Their size and unmaneuverability made the craft vulnerable to rapidly improved planes. Even armed with machine guns below and on top, they were virtually helpless. Lt. Leefe Robinson, who shot down the first dirigible over England, said, "There really was nothing to it, for once the airship is detected, it's a goner. I only had to climb above it, open fire, and drop hand grenades."

By the end of 1917, the bombing raids had stopped, but the big craft were still useful for submarine scouting and escorting convoys. They were sometimes launched from carriers, and toward the end of the war, the United States and England tried combining the range of the dirigible and the maneuverability of the plane by launching the plane from the airship.

1923

Tragedy in Thunderstorm Outmoded rules in the Gordon Bennett race forced gas balloonists to take off from Brussels on time, despite a thunderstorm. Lightning bolts killed five contestants and injured three others.

1933

New High The first official American ascent into the stratosphere was made on November 30, from an airport near the Goodyear Zeppelin Airship Dock in Akron, Ohio. Flying the balloon, called *A Century of Progress,* were the Navy's Lt. Comm. T. G. (Tex) Settle and Major C. Fordney of the Marine Corps, with instruments to measure cosmic rays. Also, in one of the first life-science experiments, plant-disease spores were taken up to see how high altitudes would affect them.

They set a new record at 61,237 feet.

1934

New High With Complications The U.S. Army Air Corps and the National Geographic Society jointly sponsored two scientifically important flights, *Explorer I* and *II.*

For the first, two and a third acres of fabric were stitched and glued together for what was to be the largest balloon ever—3 million cubic feet. Then a sheltered launch site not too near the ocean had to be found—and was—in the Black Hills of South Dakota. This Stratobowl was perfectly suited for balloon launching and has often been used since then.

With the aid of a large ground crew and the National Guard, the three aeronauts (Capt. Albert W. Stevens, Capt. Orvil A. Anderson, and Maj. William E. Kepner) cast off on July 28. They were busy monitoring their scientific instruments until 60,613 feet, when there was a bang over the gondola. Glancing up, they saw a large rip in the bottom of the balloon.

The craft plummeted earthward, the crew frantically throwing out weight as they sank. Stevens says they "could have disposed of the ballast much more rapidly if we had hurled it out in bulk, but at no time during the flight was anything thrown out in a way that might injure people on the ground."

The large gondola of *Explorer I*, a joint venture of the U.S. Army Air Corps and National Geographic Society, is prepared for its historic launch in 1934. (National Air and Space Museum, Smithsonian Institution)

All three men finally parachuted safely to earth, carrying their instruments and new and valuable data about the atmosphere.

October 23, Jeanette Piccard, "the first woman in space," piloted the *Century of Progress* balloon to a height of 57,559 feet.

1935

Repeat Flight On November 11, Anderson and Stevens ascended in *Explorer II* to a new record of 72,395 feet, or 13.7 miles, which was not to be beaten for more than twenty years and which proved that life could be sustained in the stratosphere.

1937

Hindenburg Down The explosion of the *Hindenburg* on May 6, was the final straw in a series of dirigible disasters and spelled the extinction of the beasts as passenger carriers.

High tension wires, volatile hydrogen, and storms had long plagued the rigid airships, but their luxury, stability, and speed (two days to cross the Atlantic versus a week on a ship) kept passengers coming. The German-made *Graf Zeppelin* made many safe trips, including one around the world in 1929, giving people confidence in the new ship, *Hindenburg.*

On May 4, ninety-seven passengers set off from Germany, heading for New York in luxurious though lightweight surroundings. A reporter present for the landing described what happened.

> The explosion started amidships, and was immediately followed by another explosion aft. More now followed in rapid succession . . . immediately after the first explosion the airship was transformed into a sea of flames. . . . We saw passengers . . . begin to jump from the airship to escape the flames. They fell helter-skelter on the ground. Some tried to crawl away, others remained motionless and unconscious. It was a terrifying sight.

Sixty-one people survived. Sabotage was suspected but never proved. The reputation of dirigibles was severely damaged.

1940–1945

World War II Balloons were not a major factor in World War II, but blimps were not completely discarded, and the U.S. Navy used 150 for sub hunters and convoy escorts.

For the English, barrage balloons were used as a barrier along the southern coast of England. Some 2,000 of them were tethered on steel cables as a deterrent to air assaults, forcing enemy planes to fly too high for bombing accuracy.

The Japanese came up with the plan of sending more than 1,000 unmanned balloons toward the United States west coast, armed with bombs. The news of those few which succeeded in reaching our shores was withheld, and the Japanese did not repeat the experiment.

1956

New High Lifting off from Rapid City, South Dakota, Lt. Comms. Malcolm D. Ross and Lee Lewis reached 76,000 feet in their *Strato Lab I.*

1957

New High Air Force Capt. Joseph W. Kittinger, Jr., set a new unofficial world altitude record of 96,000 feet.

New High The U.S. Air Force and the Winzen Corporation of Minneapolis joined in the preparations for *Manhigh II,* one of the most thoroughly scientific balloon ascents ever made.

In the capsule was Maj. David Simons, USAF, who could control his flight but was subject to ground-control directions. This was the first time ground control was used, setting a precedent for NASA's astronauts.

Simons was up for a record thirty-two hours and 101,516 feet, where he gathered much medical and biophysical data. He also taped many observations on the beauty of his flight. He described his gossamer balloon as being "like a lady holding on to her skirt—it drapes down so gracefully. The raveled edges wave very, very gently in the breeze."

1960

New High On August 16, Captain Kittinger, in a pressurized suit, ascended in *Excelsior III* in an open gondola to a height of almost twenty miles (102,800 feet) and then jumped out for the longest parachute jump ever made.

Falling away on his back, he saw "a beautiful balloon in a beautiful black sky *[and]* had the sensation of lying still, while the balloon raced away." His free fall ended at 17,500 feet, when he opened his main chute. The entire jump lasted thirteen minutes.

The Montgolfier Returns On October 22 in Sioux Falls, South Dakota, Ed Yost successfully launched *Vulcoon,* the first modern montgolfier incorporating a rip-resistant nylon envelope and safe propane-fired heating system. The flight started a new era in hot air ballooning.

1961

New High Malcolm D. Ross and Victor A. Prather, Jr., reached an altitude of 113,700 feet in a 10,000,000-cubic-foot balloon launched from a Navy aircraft carrier.

First Aero Club The Balloon Federation of America (BFA) was formed as the official aero club of the United States, its main aims the safety, enjoyment, and advancement of sport ballooning and the promotion of friendship among aeronauts worldwide.

1968

OK From FAA The FAA approved hot air balloon-type designs submitted by manufacturers Raven Industries and Don Piccard, paving the way for regular production of certified sports balloons for the American consumer.

1970

Indianola The First National Hot Air Balloon Championship was held in Indianola, Iowa. Winner of the inaugural race: Frank Pritchard of Flint, Michigan.

1972

Albuquerque The first Albuquerque, New Mexico, Balloon Fiesta was held. Over the years this event has grown to become the largest single assembly of sport balloons, recently attracting more than four hundred balloons.

1973

First World Hot Air Race The first World Hot Air Balloon Championship was held in Albuquerque, New Mexico, attracting 142 balloons from seventeen nations. Winner of the inaugural: Dennis Floden of Flint, Michigan.

First Cross Country Noted publisher and maverick capitalist Malcolm Forbes became the first aeronaut to fly America coast-to-coast in a continuous succession of flights using the same balloon throughout.

The *Château de Balleroy* (named after Forbes' digs in Normandy, France) was built by ballooning pioneer Ed Yost and measured sixty-five feet high and fifty-eight feet wide with a capacity of 95,000 cubic feet. The envelope contained an aluminized inner layer to aid heat retention and prolong flights. Forbes took the craft as high as 17,000 feet in the thirty-three days it took him to cross the continent in a total of twenty-one consecutive flights.

1975

First Across Lake Michigan On January 17, Paul Woessner, Jr., and Steve Neulander became the first to cross Lake Michigan. The flight, in a S-55A hot air balloon called *Magnificent Ratiteur* left from Palwaukee Airport in Wheeling, Illinois, and finished in a snow-covered field near South Haven, Michigan, three hours later.

1976

Bicentennial Flight In January of the Bicentennial year, seventy-year-old Constance Wolf lifted off from in front of Independence Hall in Philadelphia to commemorate the first United States manned ascent by Pierre Blanchard in 1793. Wearing bright red, she sailed for an hour in her helium balloon, but missed Blanchard's landing spot by fifteen miles.

(Robert Forbes)

(Forbes Magazine, Balloon Ascension Division)

Forbes magazine President and editor in chief Malcolm S. Forbes is shown in 1973 as he piloted *Château de Balleroy* over eastern Virginia in the final leg of his record transcontinental flight.

1978

Double Eagle II On August 17, *Double Eagle II* completed the first Atlantic balloon crossing, touching down in Miserey, France. The historic flight lasted 137 hours and covered 3,150 miles.

First Professional Balloon Racing Circuit The first professional hot air balloon racing circuit was organized. Called the Great American Balloon Races, it sponsored races in seven different cities in its first year, attracting a total audience estimated at several hundred thousand.

1979

Industry News The first trade group for balloon makers, the U.S. Balloon Manufacturers Association, was proposed.

Gordon Bennett Is Back The Gordon Bennett race for gas balloonists was reestablished after a hiatus of four decades. Los Angeles physicist and balloon enthusiast Tom Heinsheimer was behind the revival of the race, which tests the distance capabilities of gas balloons and their pilots.

Cross-Country Nonstop Stops Artist Vera Simons, scientist Rudolf J. Englemann, and eye surgeon Lawrence L. Hyde attempted to become the first to complete a nonstop manned balloon flight across the continental United States. Their 140-foot high clear-plastic helium balloon, the *Da Vinci Trans-America*, made it over the Rockies, and through the plains, a total of 1,380 miles, but was brought down rudely in thunderstorms in an Ohio soybean field. Simons broke her leg during the landing.

Freedom Flight Succeeds On September 15, two East German families flew over the "death strip" between the two Germanies in a homemade hot air balloon and landed twenty-eight minutes later in freedom.

1980

Father-Son Flight On May 12, *Double Eagle II* aeronaut Maxie Anderson and his son Kris, age twenty-three, made the longest overland voyage in a balloon, traveling 3,100 miles in four days and covering a straight-line distance of 2,817 miles from launch near San Francisco to landing outside Matane, Quebec, Canada. Their helium balloon *Kitty Hawk* stood seventy-five feet high.

Chapter Four

Portrait of the Artist as an Aeronaut

So far we have sketched in the various dimensions of ballooning, explained the difference between gas balloons (the charlières) and hot air balloons (the mont-golfiers), and provided a whirlwind tour of the ups and downs in ballooning in America over the past two centuries, including the present time, which is very much "up." We are in the midst of a ballooning boom.

But what about the balloonist himself? What makes today's aeronaut tick? What are the people who are in this sport really like? What are the common traits that distinguish this lot of fliers, who love to wander the skies aimlessly?

The first thing to be said is that balloonists are ruggedly and lastingly individual, and therefore it is extremely risky to generalize about what sort of personality and character they may collectively possess. Few of them are likely to admit to sharing *anything* in common with other balloonists. They are by definition their own men.

Yet there are some features that appear and reappear in the makeup of contemporary American balloonists. We do not think we are stereotyping the

(Penn Mutual Insurance Company)

Blanchard

From the early days of ballooning (the eighteenth-century's Blanchard) to the present (*Double Eagle II's* Ben Abruzzo), all aeronauts have had in common character, perseverance, imagination, and courage.

(Jay Hoey)

The marked individuality of the typical balloonist shows up in his distinctive flying uniform, in the color and design of his balloon—and sometimes even in the manner in which he travels when on the ground. (Otis Imboden)

class of balloonists by singling out for praise those features that make their customs and attitudes so lively and interesting.

It should be said at the outset that the balloonist is not necessarily a he. Women have been flying in balloons, not just as passengers but as pilots, for almost as long as men have. The first female pilot, and a very good one, was Jeanne Garnerin, and she and her husband, André, served Emperor Napoleon in that capacity. They were succeeded as "official aeronaut" by Sophie Blanchard, widow of aeronaut Jean Pierre Blanchard (who had been the first to fly a free balloon in America in 1793). Madame Blanchard made over fifty ascents in and around Paris until, tragically, she died in a balloon accident at age forty-five.

In England during the Victorian Age, it was Mrs. Margaret Graham who led the way in distaff ballooning. She shocked England not only by flying her own balloon, but by taking her three daughters along for the ride, and she persisted in her career for over forty years. Other notable women balloonists include Elsie Garnerin, who not only piloted her balloon but parachuted from it on some forty occasions, Käthe Paulus of Germany, who made a phenomenal 516 ascents and 197 parachute jumps during 1893–1909, and Jeannette Piccard, who rode a balloon to 57,579 feet on October 23, 1934, a record no other woman has yet surpassed.

In modern sport ballooning, physical size and strength are not factors in launching and operating safely, and as a result the number of women pilots today is on the rise. Many are busy setting or shooting for altitude and distance records; some are making contributions in the field of scientific research, while others, like Vicki Harrison, are piloting company balloons for such corporations as Westinghouse, as part of their marketing programs. John Wise may well have been correct when he observed a century ago, "Woman, when really determined, seems to be more daring than man."

In any event, the characterization below applies equally to men *and* to women aeronauts.

The balloonist is independent. Perhaps because he has had to be so resourceful and self-reliant in the course of his ballooning career, the modern American aeronaut is a man who insists on thinking for himself. He is therefore not happy when others attempt to tell him what to think, and will occasionally utter antiestablishment thoughts. It is not that he is against government (indeed, as a rule, he is a patriotic soul) but he doesn't like to get red tape and runarounds from the bureaucracy.

He's wary of things getting overorganized, and has several short speeches on hand for instant delivery if the subject comes up. When he attends meetings with fellow balloonists, he invariably makes it clear that he has a somewhat different opinion on how a certain race should be organized or where

Ballooning can be easily mastered by women as well as by men, and numerous women have become involved in the sport. Vivacious Vicki Harrison is a professional pilot who has toured the country on behalf of a new light bulb product from Westinghouse. (Raven Industries, Inc.)

a certain rally should be held or how the trail rope should be coiled in the bottom of the basket or what is the best month to fly the Rockies.

There's always been an independent streak in the aeronaut. In 1789, one penned this bit of mildly anticlerical whimsy for his local paper:

Our learned Divines their Flocks advise,
By fervent prayers to seek the skies;
The Aeronauts, with less devotion,
Condemn this antiquated notion,
And strive with songs and merry tunes;
To float to Heaven in Air Balloons.

Yet, for all his independence, the modern American aeronaut will be the first to come to the support of other balloonists if they need him to help with a launch or serve on the chase crew. And for all his distaste of things organized he himself is tremendously well organized when it comes time to launch his own balloon. He directs his ground handlers and chase crew with an economy of language that Captain Kirk of Starship *Enterprise* might have envied. He causes a thousand small particular acts to be made in the exact order needed, to ensure a safe and spectacular lift-off and another happy voyage.

The balloonist is proud. The balloonist may earn his living as lawyer, teacher, accountant, salesman, contractor, mechanic, business executive, butcher, baker or candlestick maker, but deep down he is a bit of an aristocrat. Ballooning itself sets him apart and above. It's natural that he should identify with fox hunting, that gloriously English exercise in ritual and privilege—which like ballooning also requires that you get up early (to take advantage of the light winds), carefully prepare your equipment, and set forth on a trip whose exact course and destination no one knows until it is achieved.

Being proud, the balloonist worries that his chosen avocation will get too crowded. He worries that someday all the "Joneses" will have balloons, too.

Yet, at the same time, he works hard to advance the art and science of his sport so that newcomers will be safely introduced, instructed, and launched.

Being proud, the balloonist is something of a loner.

Yet, he is terribly and incurably sociable. Hardly a nice weekend goes by that he doesn't round up family or friends, race off to a launch site, fly, then gather later at a landing site to crack out the beer or champagne and finally repair with everyone to a local inn for a hearty breakfast.

And when he's not flying with friends and families, he's meeting in groups that have names like the Lighter-Than-Air Society, the Armadillo Aeronauts

Balloon and Breakfast Society, and Roswell's Imperial Society for the Enjoyment of Roaring Soaring, acronym RISERS.

The balloonist is romantic. He thrives on the visual feasts provided by sunrise, sunset, lakes and mountains, seashores and cityscapes. He leans toward a nonmaterialistic explanation for how and why the universe operates—even though his craft of flying depends on a perfect understanding of physical laws. In fact, whenever he flies, he becomes obsessed with technical details—the reading on his altimeter, the temperature inside his envelope, the amount of fuel left in his tanks, the response of his craft in the wind, the total weight of his passengers, the weight of rarefied air within and the weight of the air immediately without, moving with the envelope and contributing to the overall mass.

He flies his balloon with his scientific side, but he decorates it with his romantic side. That is why his balloon carries the image of Don Quixote or Icarus or the Great Pumpkin

He is a romantic in his dress. He is Phileas T. Fogg, or Charles Lindbergh, or Eddie Rickenbacker, or the Red Baron, or he sports the "THIS IS HOUSTON CAN YOU READ ME" jumpsuit look of the 1960s' NASA astronauts. In any case, he consciously allies himself in his dress with the best of the men of the sky who have gone before.

Yet, for all his romanticism, the modern American aeronaut is a realist. He doesn't pretend he himself can fly, or that the people on the ground are looking up at him and not at his balloon. And he is not evasive or solemn in the face of adversity. He treats his miscues with just the right degree of levity. An accomplished Florida pilot we know has just the right tone when he tells this story on himself. It all happened when some unexpected winds blew him suddenly in the direction of high-voltage lines, marring what had been until then a routine but pleasant flight. His attempt to gain altitude by applying heat was not in time, and he ran into the lines. Voltage arced noisily through the craft, and the balloon, finally responding to the heat that had been applied earlier, suddenly shot upward. It went through a few more highly erratic maneuvers before making a sudden sharp descent—and landing with a thump directly on the pitcher's mound of a deserted Little League baseball diamond.

A man on the ground witnessed the entire chain of events. When the flight had terminated, he came running from his car. He approached the shaken balloonist, still in his basket on the pitcher's mound, and shook his hand vigorously. "That was the finest display of aeronautics I have ever seen!" the stranger declared. And to show his admiration, he gave the pilot, who suddenly realized the man thought he had landed on the pitcher's mound on purpose, a jar of Smucker's jam, then rushed off.

Charles Dollfuss (right), one of the great and beloved figures in twentieth-century gas ballooning worldwide, is shown being quizzed by Don Kersten, former BFA president. (Raven Industries, Inc.)

Charles Dollfuss, the most famous French balloonist of the twentieth century, displayed a similar humorous vein whenever he concluded a lecture on aerial safety. He would reach into his vest and produce a miniature bottle of brandy, and hold it up for the audience to see. When asked what the bottle was for he would reply:

"If one is inadvertently thrown from his balloon, he has just time for a *little* brandy."

Chapter Five

Getting Together— the Social Life of an Aeronaut

A balloon flight is a sociable experience. For all the solitude and special quiet achieved riding high through the sky, the balloonist knows he launches with the help of others, and, after landing, puts himself and his gear together again with the help of others as well.

The primary social relationship in ballooning is that between pilot and crew. There is a great unspoken affection between the two. The pilot is grateful to have many helping hands around as he prepares the launch. Once aloft, he is conscious of and grateful for the diligence with which the chase crew observes and follows him on earth.

The members of the ground crew, for their part, are pleased to have been able to play a part in the success of any flight, and, feeling responsible for some of the preparations and success, feel a part of the flight as well. When the balloon

Balloon rallies and races are always
exciting, never more so than at lift-off
and (especially in high winds) landing.

soars evenly in good conditions, the ground-crew members soar a bit with it. When trouble is encountered in a flight, the ground-crew member suffers with pilot and passengers. When the balloon lands safely at the end of the journey, pilot, passengers, and crew are joined in one invisible embrace.

Postflight partying may involve the occasional commemorative champagne, or a case of beer and a picnic basket, or simply rushing out for a big breakfast before heading for work.

Another social dimension of ballooning is dictated by the fact that balloonists invariably end their flights on someone else's property. It takes a tactful and honest concern for the rights of others, particularly the landowners and their property, to explain how you came to have landed on this front lawn or in that cornfield. An impudent or haughty balloonist is one who has failed to understand that responsibility.

Another line of social communication exists between the balloonist and the rest of the public whose attention he manages to attract in the course of his trip. Balloonists flying at five hundred feet can carry on conversations, albeit brief ones, with people on the ground below, and the smart ones do, making friends as they fly by. The strategy is a simple one: if you've set someone's dog to barking or horse to bolting into a gallop, you're much more likely to be forgiven if you greet that someone in a friendly way.

On earth, both at the launch and landing sites, contact with the public is even more direct. The curiosity and delight of strangers to ballooning is something the high-class aeronaut, like the professional athlete signing autographs for kids, quickly learns to be patient with. He never acts bored, though he may have heard the same questions and comments a hundred times before, and he is always aware that these people have been touched by the same spark that, perhaps long ago, turned him on, too. The usual questions and comments from a warm but naive public are these:

"Are you making a movie?"
"Say, this would make a great tent!"
"What happens if you run out of gas?"
"How fast does it go?"
"Where are you going?"
"Where did you come from?"
"What's it like up there?"
"What happens if you get a hole in the bag?"
"What happens if a bird runs into you?"
"How do you steer it?"
"But what does it *do*?"

Above and beyond these basic forms of social intercourse intrinsic to ballooning, there are local and regional ballooning events, often sponsored by

Whether in a city park, way out in the open spaces, or at a suburban high school athletic field, balloons always bring out the crowds.

A festive picnic atmosphere prevails even though the balloonists themselves take their preparations for racing quite seriously. (Sky Promotions)

ballooning clubs, and national races and rallies, and all these are primarily social events. The BFA national hot air balloon championships are held every August in Indianola, Iowa, and have attracted balloons in excess of three hundred and crowds as large as 80,000. The center of activity during the races is the balloon field located on Simpson College campus in town. The event is sponsored by the Balloon Federation of America, which also holds a variety of meetings and seminars during the week.

The largest gathering of balloons anywhere occurs every fall in Albuquerque, New Mexico. This is the Albuquerque Balloon Fiesta, and "fun flying" and friendship are the main goals of the ten-day-long celebration.

The town has apparently had a long tie to the sport. Local authorities have it that a balloon ascension took place here on July 4, 1882. A local saloonkeeper went up in a balloon, inflated with gas from the city's coal-gas system.

Nowadays the town's claim to ballooning fame, in addition to the fiesta, is the fact that among the one hundred or so resident balloonists, many of whom are outstanding pilots in their own right, are the three men who crossed the Atlantic in *Double Eagle II*. The weather is also favorable to ballooning nearly year-round, with clear skies and calm winds the rule.

This helicopter view shows a mass ascension in Albuquerque, New Mexico, annual site of the largest balloon rally in the world. (Otis Imboden)

Solitary summer flying in the nation's capital. (Wide World Photos)

The event has been held every year since 1972, and now more than four hundred hot air balloons show up for the festivities and various racing events.

The best-known balloon event is the Hare and Hound. This is known in the Southwest as the Coyote-Roadrunner race. One balloon is the Roadrunner. It takes off first, and the pilot uses every trick in the book to try to fool the other balloons, otherwise known as Coyotes. The Roadrunner pilot goes up or down to catch a different wind and heads off in a totally new direction. Then, he can change altitude, catch a new wind, and change direction again.

The Coyote balloons chase the Roadrunner and try to land as close to it as possible. The pilot who lands closest wins.

The other major balloon competition involves dropping markers onto a target. The pilot, after taking his balloon a required distance upwind from the target, is free to launch his balloon at a site of his choice. He must maneuver the balloon, changing altitude as necessary to find winds in the right direction, and get as close to the target as possible. Then the pilot drops a marker. The closest marker to the target determines the winner. In Albuquerque, pilots play this game with tumbleweeds, a commodity not hard to find there.

In a similar competition, the target is a numbered grid, which is used to play a giant game of blackjack. Each pilot, aiming drop markers at numbered squares, attempts to score 21.

Another newer race, the Elbow Bender, measures a pilot's ability to ascend and descend at certain, fixed points. Each pilot flies from the launch area and attempts to *achieve the greatest change of direction* during the flight. Each pilot drops two markers in the sequence written on the markers. The best score is that which shows the greatest change of flight angle, 180 degrees being the best. Where one observed mark is in violation of a rule, the pilot's score is penalized 1 degree for each fifty feet of infraction. Where both markers violate a rule, the pilot receives a zero score. Landing is at pilot's discretion, not less than 1,500 feet from the second mark.

Other balloon competitions include tests in precise altitude flying, using a barograph for scoring, a Jack-in-the-Box race where pilots rush to inflate their balloons the fastest and fly a set distance away from the target, and even an airborne scavenger hunt.

Launchings take place every day during the fiesta and usually involve at least a hundred balloons each. On the predawn drive to the site, which is north of the city, you invariably spot one or two illuminated balloons up for a night flight. On a typical day (when as many as 30,000 people converge to watch the ascensions) the concession stands sell 2,500 pieces of gringo bread, forty cases of beer, fifty gallons of coffee and 4,000 rolls of film—all before 9 A.M.

Chapter Six

Tripping: No Two Flights Are Ever the Same

A balloonist takes off from New Jersey, floats across Manhattan (to the astonishment of office workers staring out their windows and to the delight of local all-news radio broadcasters), then floats along Long Island Sound at altitudes as low as two hundred feet for a while, landing at last on a sandbar behind a factory in Bridgeport, Connecticut, where he promptly is ticketed for parking in an unauthorized space.

Such is the unexpected quality of nearly every flight made in a balloon, and certainly one of the reasons it holds so much charm and magnetism for participants. "We don't know where we're going to go until we get there," balloonists are always saying.

Tripping in a balloon is what the sport is all about, and in this chapter we would like to give you a taste of some of the eventful and unusual things that befall the ordinary balloonist on ordinary days. The truly spectacular achievements of those consciously striving for high adventure are left for a later chapter.

CROSS-COUNTRY IN CAROLINA

Balloonists Bill Meadows and Jim Knight set forth from western North Carolina to reach the Atlantic shoreline. It took them nine weeks, and thirty-one individual balloon flights, but they covered the 376 miles to the beach, and experienced a wide variety of impressions, experiences, and flying conditions.

They saw all sorts of people. Some called them fools and got mildly upset—there's something about the loud and crowd-drawing arrival of a balloon that disturbs men and women who are committed to a more staid daily life. But most of the people were happy and laughing. From on high the balloonists could see them sipping RC Cola in front of country stores and one-pump gas stations, or roaring in the stands in football games. They saw corn being picked, soybeans harvested, cotton chopped, tobacco auctioned off at local loose floors.

There were a few problems along the way:

Flying en masse in winter near the Colorado Rockies. (Wide World Photos)

One day's flight ended suddenly when winds picked up in a cornfield. During the rough landing the basket plowed a furrow in the field 120 feet long.

Another time they were shot at by someone with a .22.

Still another day, near the state capital in Raleigh, with the governor himself aboard, they were obliged to choose among three possible landing sites or risk the danger of flying over the city. The sites were the state prison to the left, the state mental hospital straight ahead, and the city dump below and to the right. They landed in the dump.

"Every balloonist should try at least once to go cross-country for several hundred miles, trying to hit a target of some sort," the pilots concluded after their own trip is over. "After he's tried, he will agree with us that he doesn't want to do it again soon . . . one should just ride in balloons, not try to go someplace with them!"

FLIRTING WITH FLORIDA THUNDER

Promotional balloon flights frequently are arranged for times not ideal for ballooning, and can lead to difficulties otherwise avoidable.

One such flight occurred recently on the Fourth of July in Florida. A corporation hired the balloonist to go up in the afternoon as part of a festival program. The money was right and surface winds were out of the south at about three knots, with slight gusts as high as six knots.

At first all went well. The takeoff was uneventful. The balloon moved northward at about four knots, zigzagging over the interstate highway. In forty-five minutes the balloonist and his passengers were ready to land. They came to a large parking lot that would be suitable, but decided to press on just a little more because there was an even more suitable grassy landing area up ahead.

Then they noticed the thunderheads in the sky no more than ten miles to the northwest. Almost at once their flight reversed direction from north to south. The storm literally reached out and grabbed hold of the balloon. The pilot vented and began a fast descent, hoping to land at the cloverleaf of the interstate directly below. At the lower altitude he found out how fast they were moving—at least twenty knots. The wind pushed the balloon nearly into the path of a speeding trailer truck. The pilot blasted his burners to get higher.

Rain started coming down in buckets, reducing visibility to half a mile at most. Lightning popped all around; they heard the thunder almost as soon as they saw the lightning. Finally they sailed through the storm. As visibility cleared, the pilot found two stately grain elevators directly ahead—and put on more heat. After that, encountering calm conditions at last, he began another descent. Then a powerful gust of wind walloped them once more, throwing pilot and passengers to the floor and jerking the envelope so violently that for a long, long moment it was actually parallel to the ground.

Finally they landed—hard but safely. Moments later, the storm which they had sailed through caught up with them. Having knocked them to the ground, it now proceeded to soak them thoroughly.

THREADING THE NEEDLE OF THE ST. LOUIS ARCH

Nikki Caplan is a native St. Louis balloonist who had long wished to pilot her balloon through the majestic arch called the Gateway to the West.

One day Nikki got the chance—she received permission to launch from the Jefferson National Expansion Memorial grounds, at the base of the Arch. It was to be a preliminary check to see how suitable the launch site might be for future balloon events.

Winds were minimal that day, but the area is notoriously unpredictable. Eddies of the river and cross currents flowing through the tall city canyons mingle at the Arch site to form vortex swirls and shears around the giant stainless-steel legs.

She launched from a spot under and to the west of the Arch, planning on a gradual rise to pass under and through the legs. But as the balloon approached a point directly beneath the Arch, a vortex of air pulled it to the right. The balloon bounced off the north leg, at about 250 feet above the ground. But it was a glancing blow, and moments later the needle was safely threaded.

IN SEARCH OF AMERICA

After three months of flying a cross-section of America's cultural and national resources, Bob Waligunda set down his red, white, and blue balloon in Central Park, New York City, against the backdrop of the world's most famous skyline.

An incredulous passerby stopped to help him gather the nylon folds together and remarked, "It's so beautiful, it ought to have a name, like a ship."

"It does," replied Bob. "It's the *America*."

The series of flights began on a barge on the ocean off San Francisco, with fellow aeronauts Brent Stockwell and Tom Green and Bob's brother Bill, chase-crew chief, inflating the balloon, a Raven S-50, in preparation for a never-before attempt—a flight across the Golden Gate Bridge. After the successful ascent, Bob drifted between the towers as he passed over the bridge, greeting wondering sailboats, en route to his first landing—in a tree—on Angel Island.

On his next flight, he sailed through the hills of Livermore and Antioch, famous for its wine, when skydivers suddenly appeared with chutes bursting all around the aerostat.

Past Lake Tahoe and into the Nevada desert, Bob next set down in a Nevada ghost town and communicated with the spirit of the Old West, visiting the church, the cemetery, and the saloon.

After a brief stop in Las Vegas, he proceeded to the Grand Canyon. In another ballooning first, he spanned the vastness of the canyon, dropping across the rim and down into its depths, fighting the updrafts and downdrafts, and finally rising above the North Rim, where a thirty-five-mile-an-hour landing tested his aeronautic skills to the utmost.

Next he traveled south and east over ancient Indian pueblos and into New Mexico. He landed at a commune called Lama and spent a week, joining in communal work and exchanging ideas and challenging concepts.

His next obstacle was the Rockies. Bob failed in his first attempt to cross these mountains, being knocked down by a fast-approaching thunderstorm. On the second attempt he was caught in a downdraft and crash-landed into the side of a snowy peak, unhurt, and was rescued by two Army Huey helicopters. He finally got over on the third try, with the skyline of Denver greeting him.

He took the *America* to South Dakota, and flew it past Mount Rushmore into the gorgeous Black Hills and landed at the base of Crazy Horse Mountain Memorial, soon to be South Dakota's most famous landmark. The mountain, being transformed into a gigantic 555 foot-high statue of Chief Crazy Horse, is a tribute to the Indian, with an Indian university, museum, and medical center at its foot. He spent a week with its sculptor Korczak Ziolkowski, working on the mountain and living at Crazy Horse, discussing with Korczak the sculptor's reasons for this intense dedication.

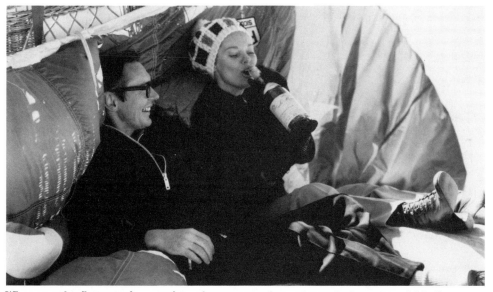

Wherever the flying is done and in whatever numbers, the end of a successful balloon trip is usually celebrated with a champagne toast. (Otis Imboden)

Bob's next flight took him over the Great Plains of Kansas, past the oil wells and grain elevators and over the massive combines as they harvested their golden crop. From the plains it was down south and across the Mississippi into the bayous of Louisiana, and out into the Gulf of Mexico, where he landed on a workboat on its way to an oil rig. Invited out to the rig, he learned how oil is brought up from offshore oil rigs as he spent a few days living and working with the roughnecks and roustabouts, thirty miles from shore.

Taking off from a helicopter platform, Bob headed for shore, only to run out of his fuel supply of propane. He was forced to ditch in the Gulf. Cajun fishermen, piloting a shrimp boat, watched his rapid descent and offered their assistance. They took him to Delcambre, the shrimp port of Louisiana, where he dried his balloon, met up with brother Bill, refueled, and headed north up the Mississippi.

This flight took him over the bluegrass horse country of Kentucky, crossing the Ohio River as the *Delta Queen* paddled beneath him, and stopped at a jazz festival to spend the day.

The final launch took place outside New York and ended with a picture-perfect touchdown in the park.

Did Waligunda find America in his three-month jaunt in a balloon?

"I found a lot of Americas, and every one of them was worth the trip."

Chapter Seven

Going for It—
the Record Makers
and Breakers

Daring to balloon where no man or woman has ballooned before—that is the ultimate call to adventure in ballooning, and it is the one area of the sport where risk to life and limb is sometimes very high and very real indeed.

The personal motives of the balloonists who embark on potentially dangerous flights, in order to set records, vary enormously.

Not long ago artist Vera Simons, scientist Rudolf J. Englemann, eye surgeon Lawrence L. Hyde, and NBC-TV cameraman Rancy Birch attempted to become the first aeronauts to complete a nonstop manned-balloon flight across the continental United States, in their 140-foot-high clear plastic helium-filled balloon, the *Da Vinci TransAmerica*.

The *Da Vinci* did not make it all the way to the East Coast, although the flight team did travel 1,380 miles before coming down in thunderstorms in a

The *Da Vinci* in the first leg of its record-setting trek in 1979. Oregon's Mount Hood is in the background. (Wide World Photos)

soybean field in Ohio. In the crash Vera Simons broke her leg and the three men were shaken up, though none of them sustained serious injury.

Simons, a German-born artist with an affinity for surrealism, said that for her the cross-continental jaunt was an attempt to create a "happening." She dropped sunflower and pine-tree seeds as their balloon sailed along, and also containers with messages in them that encouraged landlubbers to respond by flashing lights, communicating by ham radio, or laying out signs on the ground.

"I wanted people to be able to take part in it," she said, and she promised to incorporate any notes, letters, or photos she received from the public in a visual record of her trip. The world was her stage—at least until the storm ended the trip prematurely.

If Mrs. Simons' motives were artistic, those of her colleagues appeared to be linked more closely to personal makeup and to their perception of themselves at their current stage of life.

"Some people jog to exonerate themselves from their sins," said Dr. Hyde, a millionaire from Kansas City. "Thousands of years ago men killed lions. I like to lay my soul on the line in a balloon."

After the balloon made its rude landing in Ohio, the doctor admitted he would think twice before taking off on another cross-country balloon ride. But he also said he had gotten what he wanted from the experience—he had risked his life and hadn't died.

The third member of the *DaVinci* crew was Rudolf Englemann, a meteorologist employed by the National Oceanic and Atmospheric Administration. For a while NOAA had planned to fund Englemann's participation in the attempted crossing, including placing scientific instruments on board to collect data. When his agency withdrew that support, Englemann made the decision to go along for the ride on his own vacation. Why? "Because I believe in Santa Claus and the tooth fairy," he replied half-seriously to a reporter's question prior to the trip. At the conclusion of the trip, he was the first to say that he would like to try again.

Six months later, *Double Eagle II* aeronaut Maxie Anderson and his twenty-three-year-old son Kris flew *Kitty Hawk*, a 200,000-cubic-foot helium balloon, from San Francisco to a field two miles south of the St. Lawrence River in Quebec, Canada. The flight of the father-and-son team surpassed the earlier attempt by more than 1,000 miles. The trip was relatively uneventful, though for the last two days the aeronauts had to stay in oxygen masks at all times and lost their appetite for food. Why go to all that bother?

"I think it tests your mettle" was Maxie Anderson's succinct reply after landing. Anderson has now accumulated over 350 hours and 9,000 miles in gas balloons.

There is a wide range of challenges available for those interested in pursuing unique achievement in ballooning and making a name for themselves in the lighter-than-air record book. These challenges fall into four main categories: the struggle to go highest, to reach the greatest possible height in the atmosphere; the struggle to go farthest, to cover the greatest amount of linear distance; the struggle to cross major mountain ranges; and the struggle to cross major bodies of water. Let's look briefly at each of these.

ALTITUDE

The first dramatic assault on the upper reaches of the atmosphere occurred in 1862 when two Englishmen, balloonist Henry Coxwell (who in the course of his life would make more than 1,000 accident-free ascents) and scientist James Glaisher rose to an estimated 36,000 feet. The flight was made in a 90,000-cubic-foot balloon filled with coal gas and conspicuously free of the conveniences of the modern life-support systems now routinely available for the exploration of alien surroundings. For want of oxygen, Glaisher passed out long before the flight reached its zenith, and Pilot Coxwell nearly followed suit—he became so faint at one point that he had to operate the valve line with his teeth to prevent the balloon from going any higher.

Outfitted with space-age equipment, gas balloonists of this century have been able to ascend safely to three times the altitude of those early aeronauts. Advanced technology has made such feats almost commonplace. As a result, the "action" in altitude-record seeking has shifted to hot air balloons.

As of this writing, the current high-altitude hot air balloon flight record is held by Britisher Julian Nott. In 1980 he went up in a 375,000-cubic-foot balloon, sponsored by a British chemical company and a German brewery, to a record altitude of 55,900 feet.

Nott rode in a gondola of reinforced plastic and topped with a plastic dome that made it partially pressurized. The balloon carried three oxygen systems, and the flight lasted fifty minutes.

Not all altitude records are set in the airless reaches of the sky. Every balloon size class from AX-1 to AX-8 has its own set of records for altitude, for time aloft, and for distance, and, because each class of balloon has inherent physical limits, a sliding scale of achievement is necessary to recognize properly a balloonist's skill, perseverance, and courage.

DURATION

No one has ever been able to stay up in a hot air balloon appreciably longer than twenty-four hours. That's the nature of the beast: it depends on the non-renewable resource of propane for fuel. Gas balloons filled with helium or hydrogen are much better suited for long and long-lasting flights. Records are made and kept in both the montgolfière and charlière type of balloon, but the truly interesting achievements in this category are almost invariably those of the

The revival of the annual Gordon Bennett Race, with participants here shown in the starting gates in Los Angeles in 1979, has focused new attention on gas ballooning for distance. (Raven Industries, Inc.)

gas balloonist. The epitome of this is the James Gordon Bennett International Balloon Races.

The Gordon Bennett began in 1906 as a contest for distance among gas balloons to a maximum size of 80,000 cubic feet. At the time of the first race, launched in Paris, airplanes were still unknown and aeronautical interests were still centered on lighter-than-air craft. The first Gordon Bennett was therefore a major event, and some 250,000 spectators showed up to watch the launch of the sixteen balloons taking part in the inaugural, representing the national aero clubs of France, United States, Germany, Great Britain, Belgium, Italy, and Spain. The French were favored to win the race, but U.S. Army Lt. Frank P. Lahm was the upset victor when he found a wind that carried him north over the Channel and reached a distance of 410 miles.

Subsequently, the Gordon Bennett was held annually until 1913, discontinued during the war years, then resumed and conducted annually again through 1938, with the exception of the Depression year of 1931, when economic conditions forced its cancellation. The 1939 race was to take place on September 3 in Poland. But two days before, the city of Lvov was bombed by the Germans, and World War II began. In 1979, Los Angeles physicist and balloonist Tom Heinsheimer organized a revival of the event.

The greatest distance covered in the Gordon Bennett to date is 1,361 miles, achieved back in 1912 by the French balloonist Maurice Bienaimé. Other thousand-mile voyages have been chalked up by Alan R. Hawley of the United States (1,173 miles in 1910), Ernest Demuyter of Belgium (1,098 miles in 1920 and 1,066 miles in 1936), Zbigniew Burzynski of Poland (1,025 miles in 1935), and Antoni Janusz of Poland (1,051 miles in 1938).

The greatest amount of time spent in the air in a Gordon Bennett to date is seventy-four hours, achieved in 1980 by the *Double Eagle* balloonists Ben Abruzzo and Larry Newman. Taking off from Mile Square Park, a former World War II air strip south of Los Angeles, Abruzzo and Newman played a waiting game with the winds, hoping to find a westerly zephyr that would get them started on a possible transcontinental journey. As a result they ended up in the air a full day longer than any of the other ten balloonists in the race, all of whom allowed the prevailing winds at the time of launch to carry them north. The *Double Eagle IV* balloon traveled more miles than any other entrant, but two hundred of them were backward. Eventually winners of the 1980 event were another pair of Americans, Jerry Tepper and Corky Meyers. They flew *Cloud Dancer* 528.5 miles—all in one direction.

MOUNTAINS

"Why do you want to fly the mountain?"
　　"Because it's there."

Mountains hold the same attraction for balloonists that they do for climbers. Their extreme altitude and unstable wind conditions provide a special challenge to aeronautical skills. Since 1849, when the first balloon crossing of the Alps was accomplished, aeronauts have sought out mountain ranges for hop-skip-and-jump ascensions.

As with altitude flights, the action today in mountain ballooning is primarily with the montgolfier class. A few recent examples:

Former national ballooning champion Tom Gabel became the first to fly a balloon over the Great Smoky Mountains. During his five-hour, seventy-mile flight he was almost always lost in clouds, knocked back and forth by turbulent winds, and periodically shot up in the air by hot spots.

On August 12, 1978, Steve Hodgson became the first to fly a balloon over the Grand Teton peaks in Idaho. He did it in two stages. A preliminary flight brought him from Idaho Falls to a 9,000-foot-high ridge just short of the peaks. On the next day he flew at 12,000–15,000 feet on a course directly between the Grand and South Peaks, and eventually came down smoothly on the shore of Jackson Lake.

A much more difficult "first" was achieved by Florida attorney Kingswood Sprott in January of 1978 when he flew over the rugged Andes mountains in South America. This 70-minute flight through 18,000 to 20,000-foot peaks was the result of nearly two years of careful preparation. The flight itself was harrow-

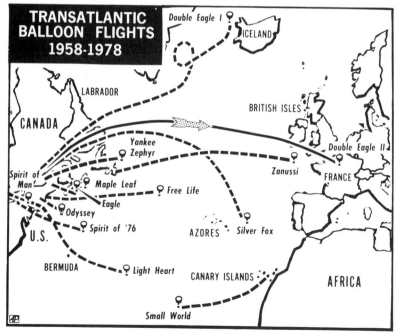

Two decades in the Atlantic challenge. (Wide World Photos)

ing, to say the least. Early on, the struggle was to achieve enough lift to clear towering rock walls and to endure wind turbulence that at one point knocked the entire body of the envelope horizontal to the ground, with the basket swinging out in the opposite direction. Then, twenty-five minutes into the flight, both burners mysteriously went out. Sprott said "Now there is total silence, blue sky and less than 2,000 feet of airspace between us and the crags we approach at 75 miles per hour. I've had moments in balloons before . . . like the top out at 5,000 feet, or the envelope splitting straight up a seam at 8,000, or even the burner frame melting in half at 30,000. But this moment stands alone. And probably it's worse for Bill (Bill Spoher, Sprott's copilot) than for me because he has nothing to do except to pray that I find an immediate solution."

After three minutes of increasingly panicky manipulations, Sprott coaxed a flame out of one of the burners, and the crisis was over. Though there were additional difficulties both with the fuel system and oxygen supply masks when the balloon climbed to 21,000 feet, they were overcome with less anxiety. Seventy minutes after lift-off, the balloon safely reached the western edge of the Argentine pampas.

OCEAN

The most galvanizing of all the ballooning challenges has been the idea of crossing the Atlantic. As we noted earlier, the great nineteenth-century American aeronauts John Wise and T. S. C. Lowe both saw the challenge and designed balloons capable of tackling the job. Though their plans resulted in flights that ended in failure, the two men did much to bring the dream into realistic focus.

The dream lay dormant in the first half of the twentieth-century, years which belonged to powered flight and the monumental dream of outer space. Then the transatlantic balloon voyage became a matter for ardent speculation once more. And soon, plots were hatched to make the dream happen at last.

This modern assault-by-balloon on the Atlantic Ocean is summarized below.

1958 Four English seamen with no real ballooning experience take off from the Canary Islands in their *Small World* balloon in an effort to cross the Atlantic going from east to west. They are forced down after 1,900 miles and put up a sail and manage to sail their gondola the rest of the way to Barbados, thus achieving the first crossing made at least in part by balloon.

The seaworthy design of their gondola is one that many subsequent attempts will imitate.

1968 Francis Brenton plans a launch from Canary Islands but his hydrogen balloon explodes during inflation.

1968 Francis Brenton tries again; this time his balloon splits open immediately after takeoff and the flight from Madeira, Spain, is aborted.

1968 Two Canadian actors, Mark Winters and Jerry Kostur, ride their 35,000-cubic-foot helium-filled balloon *Maple Leaf* from Halifax, Nova Scotia, to a splashdown in the ocean thirty-five miles southeast of Halifax.

1970 This flight, ending in tragedy, culminates the longtime dream of thirty-two-year-old Rod Anderson, a Wall Street commodities broker, and his wife, twenty-eight-year-old TV actress Pamela Brown. Neither has ever been up in a balloon, but they spend more than $100,000 to build *The Free Life* and enlist as pilot an English aeronautical engineer named Malcolm Brighton, who does have considerable experience in ballooning.

The Free Life consists of a 73,000-cubic-foot inner balloon filled with helium and an outer balloon filled with hot air and designed as a heat-exchange area for warming the helium.

Launch site is East Hampton, Long Island, New York. Amid a carnival atmosphere, with 1,500 townspeople gathered, the trio takes off at 1:40 P.M. on Sunday, September 20, and leave the coast, traveling northeast. Almost immediately there are difficulties. The burner system fails, leaving them with the capacity of a conventional gas balloon. On the following evening, a cold front develops, and they fly into a storm. Pilot Brighton reports by radio that they are going to ditch. Their ten-foot-long fiberglass/aluminum gondola had reportedly been constructed to meet such an emergency, being buoyant and equipped with a tent to keep out rain. But at the time of ditching the waves were estimated to be ten to twenty feet high and wind was blowing at twenty-five to thirty knots.

Extensive search parties fail to uncover any sign of the threesome.

1973 Bob Sparks launches his hot air balloon *Yankee Zephyr* from Bar Harbor, Maine, but within twenty-four hours the balloon meets severe thunderstorms and is forced down forty-five miles northeast of St. John's, Newfoundland. Sparks is rescued by a Canadian icebreaker.

1974 *The Light Heart* is a flotilla of ten helium balloons with a sealed fiberglass gondola suspended 190 feet beneath them. It is the brainchild of forty-eight-year-old Thomas L. Gatch, an Army Reserve colonel working at the Pentagon and a balloonist with relatively little experience.

Gatch's idea is to use a multitude of quarter-filled superpressure helium balloons that will expand to capacity when the craft reaches 36,000 feet. He designs the gondola to withstand temperatures down to 65 degrees below zero and puts on board ten days of provisions plus radio and emergency equipment.

Before a crowd of about 1,000, *The Light Heart* soars into the darkness at 7:20 P.M. on February 18 from Harrisburg International Airport. Within three hours it is over the Atlantic, traveling eastward in a seventy MPH jet stream.

One of the balloons bursts in the first hours, reducing the lifting power and thus also the duration potential. Preflight planning has specified that the flight be aborted in event of a balloon failure, but that procedure is not followed.

Gatch is forced to ride the southern edge of the jet stream, causing his flotilla to veer away from the direction of Europe and toward an area of the Atlantic seldom visited by aircraft. Last radio contact with him is on Wednesday. On Thursday morning, the balloon is reportedly sighted by a freighter somewhere west of the Canary Islands. Nothing more is seen or heard of *The Light Heart*.

1974 Bob Berger takes off from Lakehurst, New Jersey, in the *Spirit of Man*, a homemade balloon and gondola that falls apart at one mile altitude. Berger, who was not a licensed balloonist, is killed in the fall. Previously he had built three other balloons inside a high school gym, and each had fallen apart during trial inflation.

1975 Publisher Malcolm Forbes and Dr. Thomas F. Heinsheimer prepare to take off from Marine Air Terminal, Santa Ana, California, in their two-man *Windborne*, thirteen-balloon cluster, designed like the Gatch flotilla, to ride the jet stream to Europe and so avoid the Atlantic storms at lower altitudes.

Their launch on January 6 is aborted when the last six balloons lift off prematurely in a gust of wind, jerking the gondola off its launch cart. Fast action by the launch director in cutting the balloons may well have saved the lives of the two men inside the sealed gondola.

Though the flight ends in failure (says publisher Forbes, "Thirty-five yards isn't much of a record."), it was actually one of the most carefully planned efforts to date. The idea in launching from California was to give the flight a trial run across country. Then, if all had gone well, to continue flying over the Atlantic.

1975 Bob Sparks tries again, this time in *Odyssey*, lifting off from Mashpee, Massachusetts. His solo attempt is marred at the outset when his crew chief, Haddon Wood, deliberately hangs onto a drag rope at lift-off and hauls himself on board. Then, when a leak forces the balloon down 125 miles from shore, the stowaway stays with the gondola, and Sparks leaves by rescue helicopter. Later Wood claims that under admiralty law, Sparks abandoned the craft, and Wood claims it as his own. Sparks eventually recovers the gondola, only to lose it to another man by the name of Karl Thomas. Thomas, who has financed a portion of the *Odyssey* flight, shows up with a writ claiming the gondola as just compensation and saying he wants it for a transatlantic flight he is planning.

1976 Karl Thomas launches from Lakehurst, New Jersey, in a 77,000-cubic-foot balloon called *Spirit of '76* and the gondola he has repossessed from Bob Sparks.

Two days later and 550 miles out to sea, he is forced down in a thunderstorm. Spilled into the water upon ditching, he loses the gondola but manages to get his life raft. He drifts for four days without food or water until rescued by a Soviet freighter and taken to Rotterdam.

Later the sturdy gondola is recovered and returned to him.

1976 Ed Yost takes off on October 5 from Millbridge, Maine, in the *Silver Fox*, an eighty-foot-high helium balloon with a capacity of 60,000 cubic feet and a total payload weighing less than two tons.

The balloon floats northeastward over Canada, then out over the ocean. After three days of uneventful but steady progress, the *Silver Fox* runs into an air mass called the Azores high, which forces Yost south into a clockwise weather pattern that threatens to take him all the way to the Caribbean. He maneuvers for another day looking in vain for more favorable winds, then reluctantly touches down two hundred miles east of the Azores and only seven hundred miles from Portugal. He and his balloon are picked up by a West German freighter and brought into Gibraltar.

Yost flew a total of 2,740 miles in 107 hours, twenty-seven minutes, breaking the previous records of 1,896 miles and eighty-seven hours for balloons of unlimited size.

1977 Maxie Anderson reads about Ed Yost's attempted crossing in the February 1977 issue of *National Geographic* and decides he would like to try. He asks fellow Albuquerque businessman and balloonist Ben Abruzzo to join him. After months of preparation they take off on September 9 from Marshfield, Massachusetts, in *Double Eagle*, a 101,000-cubic-foot helium balloon with a V-hulled gondola, total weight 6,680 pounds. They cross Boston Bay, then Portland, Maine, then fly over Canada and Labrador before finally leaving the land mass.

The balloon is pulled northward into a giant circular air movement between Greenland and Iceland, which threatens to take them over the polar ice pack.

On the next day, because of the unexpectedly wide course they are on, lashed by freezing rain and wind and having serious radio difficulties, they decide to dump. They issue a Mayday and descend at two hundred feet per minute into twenty-five-foot waves three miles off the northwestern tip of Iceland.

A half hour later, they are rescued by an Air Force helicopter. Later on an Icelandic cutter retrieves the gondola.

1977 Dewey Reinhard and Steve Stephenson take off on October 10 from Bar Harbor, Maine, in *Eagle*, an 86,000-cubic-foot helium balloon. Reinhard, an experienced hot air balloonist who operates his own electronics business in Colorado Springs, estimates preparations for the flight involved ten months of full-time effort by his family.

Unlike previous Atlantic attempts, this flight aims to take the low road across—to stay as near to the water as possible. In the early stages there are frequent yo-yolike sudden drops that amount to collisions with the water, and the balloon is twice shaken by sonic boom by passing Concordes. Then, the transmitting equipment fails and the pair lose indispensable contact with their source of weather information in Washington, D.C.

On the third night out they are overtaken by heavy hail and rainstorms, and they make the decision to ditch. Because of the ballast floating beneath the gondola and the ten to fifteen knot winds and sixty-foot-high waves, there are problems in landing the balloon. Reinhard cuts away the envelope on impact, later quipping, "Disposing of $56,000 worth of equipment with a flick of the wrist was a traumatic experience."

The men are picked up by a Canadian Coast Guard buoy tender three hours after splashdown.

1978 Britons Don Cameron and Chris Davey take off from a baseball field near St. John's, Newfoundland on July 26 in a fourteen-foot gondola under a double balloon called *Zanussi*. The envelope consists of a helium gas cell of 15,000-cubic-foot capacity contained within a hot air balloon of 150,000 cubic feet. In spite of an eight-foot tear that develops in the gas balloon, the pair get

In 1978, the *Zanussi*, piloted by Britons Don Cameron and Chris Davey, came within 110 miles of making the first transatlantic crossing. (Wide World Photos)

more than halfway across the Atlantic by the third day. Then the continued leakage of helium and a sudden drop in the wind begin to thwart their efforts. On the fifth day, with ballast gone and still no wind, the *Zanussi* touches down in the ocean, 103 miles from the coast of France.

Cameron and Davey are picked up by a French trawler.

1978 No sooner has Maxie Anderson been rescued from the sea after the failed attempt in 1977 than he makes up his mind to try again, and he soon persuades fellow *Double Eagle* pilot Ben Abruzzo to join him. Abruzzo recruits a third crew member, hang-gliding expert Larry Newman, to serve as radio operator, and the three take off on August 11, from Presque Isle, Maine, in *Double Eagle II*. The eleven-story-high helium balloon, designed and built by Ed Yost, flies for 137 hours, six minutes and covers 4,997 kilometers before touching down in Miserey, France, on August 17. The historic crossing was actually achieved August 16 when the balloon reached landfall on the coast of Ireland, but favorable winds permitted the trio to fly across England over the Channel and into France.

Chapter Eight

Making It All Pay Off

Not long after the first manned balloon flight took place in Paris in 1783, a skeptic asked Benjamin Franklin, "What good could a balloon possibly be?"

Franklin replied, "What good is a newborn baby?"

Today, while only a small number of sports balloonists actually make a living doing what they like to do best, ballooning itself is doing a lot of good in a number of areas, and has the potential to do good in some exciting new ways, too.

With the growth of sport ballooning over the past decade, a small new industry has been created. This consists primarily of the manufacturers and their sales personnel, balloon repair stations, and pilot instructors.

The commercial uses of ballooning in advertising and promotion are by now familiar to many people. *Double Eagle* pilot Ben Abruzzo sees a continuing and expanding use of balloons in this area. "The balloon provides a relatively inexpensive advertising platform," he notes, "and apparently from the great number of commercial balloons that are now flying, the results are satisfactory to the sponsors. I believe that this area will continue to expand at a rapid rate."

Sunstat is an experimental balloon that flies using solar energy solely. (Jim Winker)

Goodyear estimates that over 150 million people see its airships in a typical year. The same kind, if not degree, of exposure is what balloons provide for the products of brewers, soft-drink bottlers and tobacco companies at such gatherings as state fairs, football games, civic festivals, and the like. Recently a race of more than a dozen commercial balloons in Philadelphia attracted an estimated 350,000 spectators. The name of the game is exposure, and though some marketing people have complained that with more and more firms using ballooning to convey their messages, the quality of the exposure is suspect, the truth is that we have not reached the saturation point, and are certainly a long way from the day when people won't bother to look up and appreciate the splendid sight of a balloon floating by.

There is a distinct possibility that the new professional balloon-racing circuits will attract the kind of sponsorship and popular fan appeal to make it a major year-long attraction. This in turn would create new jobs in ballooning and stimulate even more interest in the sport, both as a participant activity and as a spectacle for stay-at-homes and picnickers.

Industrial or developmental uses for the balloon are not figments of the imagination. A hot air balloon was recently used as a scout craft in the Canadian Arctic. A firm involved in exploration work used the balloon to observe the jagged ice ranges from aloft and find the shortest, fastest, and safest route for the firm's equipment from day to day. Helicopters or planes couldn't do the job because of the extreme expense, the problem in storing and maintaining, and also the danger when snowstorms suddenly come up.

Two potential, though questionable, heavy-lifting uses for dirigibles—balloons that are steerable airships with rigid or nonrigid fuselage—are logging and cargo carrying.

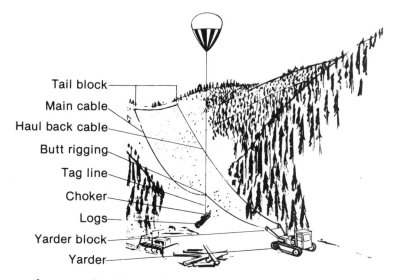

Tail block

Main cable

Haul back cable

Butt rigging

Tag line

Choker

Logs

Yarder block

Yarder

Balloons are being used for heavy-duty hauling in remote locations. Sketch depicts how this logging operation works. (Raven Industries, Inc.)

High-altitude research balloon being prepared to lift its scientific payload. (Raven Industries, Inc.)

Artists' rendering of the National Oceanic and Atmospheric Administration's future application of heavy-lift and cargo dirigibles, based on a conceptual design by Kurt Stehling and Gordon Vaeth, of NOAA, in their NOAA "Helium Horse" article. (Kurt Stehling, NOAA)

Hot air blimps are now being developed for uses in industry. (Raven Industries, Inc.)

The Navy and the U.S. Forest Service are presently working together to develop a blimp to see if airborne logging is feasible. These would replace the helicopters that are used now in logging—hauling logs by air out of areas that are inaccessible or where dragging them on the ground would be environmentally damaging.

The biggest helicopters available can lift about seventeen tons, but loggers want to go up to at least twenty-five and maybe seventy-five tons. A rotor-assisted hybrid airship that would get half of its lift from helium and half from rotors could get operating costs down to about one third the cost of the helicopters.

Offloading ships in areas where there is no port facility, or in American ports where container ships are used but often have to wait to get in to be unloaded, is another major potential use of dirigibles. Instead of coming through the Golden Gate in San Francisco, for example, a container ship offshore could be unloaded by a dirigible without even slowing down, and the cargo could be carried direct to staging areas twenty to forty miles inland, avoiding the congestion of the harbors.

Dirigibles to do such jobs would be enormous—measuring the length of three football fields, perhaps—and would have volume in cubic feet perhaps three or four times that of the early dirigibles such as the *Hindenburg* or the Navy's *Akron* and *Macon.*

So-called Third World countries could benefit enormously from balloon technology. Dr. Emilio Castanon of the Organization of American States (OAS) has produced a study containing a number of intriguing ideas for the use of dirigibles.

With their knack for maneuvering and unloading freight anywhere, blimps or dirigibles give one the chance to exploit natural resources not currently reachable by land. Dr. Castanon envisions other potential applications for the balloon-supported air vessel, including use as a floating hospital, a mobile government agency, and an instrument for soil, timber, and even population surveys.

The *potential* future for the balloons is great. They may be harnessed for sport, for entertainment, for science, or for profit, or for any and all of those combinations. Oddly enough, no matter what purpose it is put to, in the eyes of the child, artist, or poet, the balloon will always appear against the sky something quite impractical and of unusual value just for that reason.

Part Two
THE EDUCATION OF A BALLOONIST

Chapter Nine

Your First "Morning in the Sun"

In one of his broadcasts a few years ago, Paul Harvey reported on his maiden voyage in a balloon which occurred once when he had been in Albuquerque on business:

> Well I've heard tell what it's like; how when the noisy burners are actuated there is from below the chorus of a thousand barking dogs, how people really do run from their houses and look up and run back for cameras; except golfers that never look up, of course. But for a longtime airplane driver, the magic of the otherwise stillness chokes you up with a kind of reverential awe, and the windless smoothness as you ride in the air instead of through it. Gradually you become accustomed to the looking down and you begin to amuse yourself with mischievous conjecture . . . . So now I return to the soiled snow of Chicago. But that's all right, for I have had my morning in the sun, and evermore I will have only to close my eyes, and I will possess a part of the wide New Mexico skies for the rest of my life.

Predawn rendezvous at the launch site, in this case a grassy airstrip. (Phil Smith)

Other ballooning first-timers are almost always equally enraptured:

"It was like being a bird and being able to soar and hover and enjoy total freedom, escape from the world. We just got into our magic balloon and the world went away, but it continued to move as if to say, 'See what I've got, see how pretty I am, don't you want to come back?' No, no, never, I want to stay here forever."

"It was like being your own cloud."

"It was an experience in flight impossible to compare with any other. In hang-gliding or skydiving, there is always the wind and the sensation of speed; in a fixed-wing aircraft or helicopter, there is always the noise. But in a balloon there are only timeless moments of utter stillness, creating the euphoria of a dream."

But let us reconstruct in more detail, for those readers who have not yet had the experience, a typical introduction to an hour aloft in a balloon. No two experiences are ever exactly the same, but a number of thoughts and feelings repeat themselves in almost every initiate.

ARRIVAL

It is 5:45 A.M., and you have been driving for two hours. It doesn't usually take so long to get to a launch site, but you happen to live in Connecticut and the

The preflight weather check includes physical observation of existing wind conditions. (Phil Smith)

balloon pilot you have contracted to take you up operates out of Princeton, New Jersey, so the drive is necessary. In any case, a certain amount of predawn driving is the rule for would-be balloon passengers. There is always plenty of time to be with your thoughts—and drowsily to second-guess your decision to seek a chance to ride in a balloon in the first place.

After all, what does this matter to you? What can you hope to get out of something so indulgent and impractical as a ride in a balloon? How could it possibly be worth all the bother? "Would you like to ride in my beautiful balloon?" went the popular song of a few years ago. You'd never particularly liked that song, so why are you saying "yes" to it now? Why aren't you in bed with the rest of the world?

The closer you get to your destination, the more hesitant you become about the whole thing. Perhaps you've got the directions wrong and won't be able to find the agreed-upon place for rendezvous. Perhaps you've got the wrong day, and no one will be there. Perhaps you've got the right place and the right day—but suddenly have a flat tire so that the whole thing has to be called off.

But of course your directions are good, and your tires hold out, and you arrive at the tiny airstrip where you are to meet the balloonist and his crew. Dawn's flattering golden light has given the ramshackle sheds near the strip a temporary paint job, the trees are bursting with new growth, and the green grass of summer grows tall all around the parking lot into which you turn. Doubt and indecision behind you, you feel the first stirrings of anticipation. You're finally waking up.

Your pilot and another young man and a woman are leaning against the fender of a pickup truck. In the back of the truck sits the wicker gondola that you will be flying in, presumably. The pilot greets you and says:

"It's not absolutely perfect flying weather."

Dutifully you glance at the skies, wondering what perfect is. There are some strips of raggedy gray clouds moving overhead, but the sun is mostly out, so what could be wrong? If the issue were the playing of a baseball game, the game would start on schedule. But, you realize, ballooning takes place in the world of the air, a world you are not really familiar with beyond knowing it is hot or cold, raining, snowing, or sunny.

"I want you to met Vicki, who is also a pilot," says your pilot after shaking your hand. She is an attractive brunette, also dressed in a jumpsuit. "And this is Mike. He'll be driving the chase car today. The rest of the crew will be along shortly. Vicki will be flying with us today—provided you want to go up."

"Why shouldn't I?"

"We've got clouds moving in over there," the pilot points. "And the ceiling's low—we probably wouldn't be able to go much higher than five hundred feet. What do you think?"

You think, is he asking *you* to make the decision about the flight? Biding your time, you lean over the side of the pickup and stroke the leather trim on the basket. Applying pressure with your hand, you decide the basket feels reassuringly sturdy.

"Are you saying it might be dangerous to fly today?"

"Not dangerous," the pilot replies. "It's just that, for the first time up, it might not be perfect for you. On a perfect day there'd be less wind."

"What wind is that?" you say, having noticed nothing of the sort.

The pilot points out the leaves fluttering in the top of some maples in the near distance. "That means six or seven miles an hour," he says. Then he asks you to tell him what direction the wind is coming from. Studying the telltale leaves he has just used to gauge wind velocity, you decide it is impossible to know what direction the wind is coming from. The leaves are blowing every which way.

"I give up!"

"Hold your hands up this way," says the pilot. With his forearms perpendicular to the ground and his palms open, he stands and turns on his hips from one side to another, back and forth like a human radar station. "Find the place where you can feel the air on your palms," he says. You imitate him, and after rotating for a while, you do indeed become aware of gentle air movement, and you point in the direction it is coming from. "That's right," the pilot says. "Out of the south/southeast. Normally around here that means a low pressure system is moving in and with it storms. But that won't be a factor until later in the day. So what do you think?"

"I'd like to go up if we can," you say, still exuberant over your correct detection of the wind.

"Then let's do it," says the pilot with a clap of his hands. "Hop in the pickup."

PREPARATIONS

The pickup bumps along on a roundabout course, past a motley group of small single-engine planes tied to their hitching posts, then into the center of the grassy airstrip. "We'll set up in the lee of those trees over there," the pilot says on the way. "That'll protect us from any gusts of wind that come up while we're inflating the balloon."

Right behind the pickup is a van with the rest of the crew. "You can inflate and lift off with only one or two helpers in the right circumstances," says the pilot. "In fact, some experienced balloonists have figured out ways to do the whole thing solo. But it's best to have three or four people on crew. It's also more social."

Shortly, both vehicles come to a halt, everyone jumps out, and after another round of introductions and more speculation about the weather, preparation for the flight begins in earnest.

Conditions are excellent for flying, so the equipment is promptly unloaded. (Phil Smith)

The basket and an enormous canvas bag containing the envelope are lifted off the truck. While crew members occupy themselves with the latter, the pilot and Vicki concentrate on the burner system. Strapped inside the basket are two cylinders vaguely resembling a dairy farmer's milk containers. In fact they are the propane gas tanks. "You can't check your burner system too much," explains the pilot, sniffing for possible gas leaks at various valves and fittings. "The fuel itself is under pressure, so it has to be handled with respect. And the success of your flight depends on access to the fuel, so the system for burning it has to be working perfectly."

In spite of the pilot's methodical approach, you are impressed with how easy and uncomplicated it all seems. There are no lines, no tickets, no security checks, no crowds, no seat belts, no flight attendants—none of the things that make flying on a commercial airline so tedious and time-consuming.

Your first real surprise, though, comes when the envelope is pulled out of the canvas bag. You watch the two crew members assigned this duty pull and pull and pull . . . and still fabric keeps coming out of the bag. It reminds you of a magician pulling an endless string of kerchiefs out of a top hat. But at last the envelope, with its bright red and white and yellow panels, is stretched to its full length of fifty feet. You express your astonishment at how much area it covers—

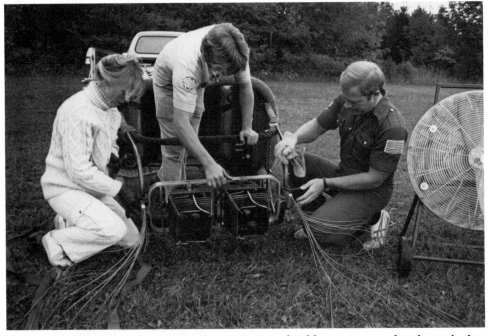

While the crewman positions burners for rigging, steel cables are removed and attached to the basket. (Phil Smith)

114 **The Education of a Balloonist**

Securing cables to the basket. (Phil Smith)

more than a good-sized swimming pool takes up. "This one's about average," says one of the crew blithely.

You walk around this average balloon and feel positively Lilliputian next to it.

The pilot and Vicki push the basket on its side so that its aluminum superstructure and the pair of burners mounted on top of the struts are pointing at the envelope. Steel cables attached to the envelope are hooked into place on the struts, connecting gondola with its lifting agent. In a few minutes, the pilot announces:

"Okay, we're ready to inflate."

One of the crew unloads what looks like a window fan from the truck and brings it over to the pilot. Actually, it is a gas-powered inflator or blower. "You can fill up the envelope without a power blower," the pilot says. "Traditionalists do it by picking up the envelope at the mouth and flapping it up and down. It takes a long time, and you need the arms of a weightlifter."

The pilot starts up the inflator, two crew members hold the mouth of the envelope open in front of the rushing air, and in a matter of minutes your second major surprise of the morning occurs. This is the sight of the balloon heaving slowly but surely into life on the field, growing like some giant Alice-in-Wonderland mushroom before your eyes.

Attaching fuel lines to burners. (Phil Smith)

The envelope is pulled out to its full length, then spread out on the ground. (Phil Smith)

The inflation fan is turned on and directed to blow cold air into the mouth of the balloon. In a matter of minutes, the envelope is half-full. (Phil Smith)

Preflight procedures include checking temperature telltales in the balloon fabric and securing the maneuvering vent. (Phil Smith)

Vicki Harrison makes sure the maneuvering vent line and rip line are not tangled, then brings the line out through the throat to attach to the basket. (Phil Smith)

Soon the balloon is a big bulbous blob, tended on all sides, as though it is a blob not fully to be trusted, by crew members. Above the noise of the inflation, you hear the pilot say, "Let's take a walk."

Next thing you know, you are taking a walk *inside* the blob. Feeling like Jonah inside the whale, you are both fearful and giddy. The envelope ripples and glows and occasionally sways from side to side in response to the morning's breezes. Not filled to capacity, it's still out of round in many spots. The pilot, study – ing the walls around him explains, "We always check the interior to be sure there are no problems."

"What kind of problems could there be?"

"Holes in the envelope, if they were large enough, could make it harder for you to contain your warm air. These vents should be double-checked to be sure they're sealed. The two lines here, one from the rip panel, and the other from the maneuvering vent, can't get tangled. And this little white telltale, which works something like litmus paper, should be checked to be sure the fabric hasn't been overheated. If it's turned black, it means the fabric may have been weakened. But as you see, this is white. Everything's cool."

Outside again, the fun really begins. The pilot situates himself between the

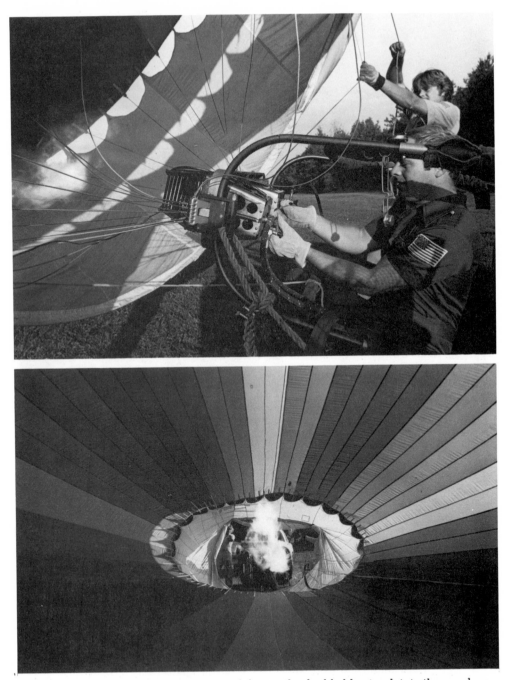

Pilot Bob Waligunda lights the burners and directs the double blowtorch into the envelope. (Phil Smith)

As the air inside the balloon is heated, it expands and soon the envelope starts to rise, pulling the basket itself upright. (Phil Smith)

basket, still on its side on the ground, and the burners. Vicki and one of the crew stand on either side, grab the mouth of the envelope, and hold it open. The burner is ignited. The pilot turns on the blast valve controlling the flow of propane. A long blue-red flame darts into being.

"Something wrong?" the pilot shouts above the roar.

"No!" you shout back.

"Your eyes have gotten bigger!" he smiles.

In fact the noise of the burner, the sight of the eight-foot-long flames and the feel of the intense heat all conspire to restore some of the doubt you were experiencing earlier in the morning.

But it is all too compelling not to stay rooted to your spot. Hot air pours into the envelope. At first nothing appears to be happening, but then you see the soft spots in the envelope begin to fill out. As the balloon nears its true rounded form, you step back from it to try to appreciate the scale of the event you are witnessing.

Then it happens. The air inside is suddenly hot enough to impart buoyancy to the balloon. It is like watching a circus elephant rise from its bed of straw. The balloon is ungainly yet monumental, and the more it rises, the more majestic it becomes.

More magic: the pilot and crew must jockey out of the way, for as the balloon reaches a vertical position, it pulls taut the steel cables and brings the basket upright of its own accord.

You find yourself shaking your head, laughing.

One of the crew shuts off the inflation fan. The pilot lets go of the trigger on his blast valve. Things are quiet again. Vicki brings over a set of gauges, which the pilot fits to a spot inside the basket. "Altimeter, variometer, and temperature gauge," he says. "Required on every flight." Then he adds in a casual tone that takes you by surprise, "Okay, why don't you get in?"

LIFT-OFF

If you're young and spirited, you might not give a second thought to the act of climbing inside a small wicker basket that sits directly under a five-story-high balloon. But if you're a bit older or have led sheltered a life, you may well ask yourself at this point, "What in God's name am I doing here?"

A few irrational thoughts may cross your mind, such as "Do balloons really go up?" "Do they ever come down?" "Is all this covered by my insurance?" "Will I need two years of therapy to get over it?" "Will I be afraid of heights and have to sit in the bottom of the basket with my eyes closed the whole time?"

Vicki joins you and the pilot, and to take your mind off your pusillanimous musings, you try to remember the lines in the nursery rhyme about three men in a tub, but to no avail.

Bob sets his altimeter to field elevation. Also on controls console are a rate-of-climb indicator, a pyrometer, and blast valves for the burners. (Phil Smith)

Crew chief delivers champagne. Then, with one more blast of the burner, the balloon is airborne. (Phil Smith)

One of the chase crew unties the handling line from the axle of the pickup truck and with Vicki's help carefully stores it in a ball on the floor of the basket. The pilot pulls the trigger on the blast valve for two short intervals. Now the crew stands around the basket with their hands on the rim.

There is a slight upward movement—or is that your imagination?

"Hands off," says the pilot.

The crew backs away from the basket. One of them—the one who earlier pooh-poohed your praise of the envelope's great size when it was being stretched out on the ground—is looking at you. Consummate actor that you are, you manage to produce a small, confident smile.

All at once, but slowly like the snail, the balloon pulls away from the face of the earth.

SAILING

The hardest part about flying in a balloon is trying to describe it accurately. Moments into your first flight, you realize this first and foremost. Your first thought is that it is like taking a slow, leisurely walk, only at treetop level instead of ground level, but you immediately realize that image is a good try, nothing more. It may be that you could make a collage out of all your previous experiences—skiing, hiking, meditating, drinking, loving, laughing—that would help you to approximate the adventure of a balloon ride, but it is doubtful.

The hour passes uneventfully. That is, there are no sudden ups or downs or twists or bumps or turns or spins. But the truth is, the hour is dense with event.

The land you are crossing is at the outer edge of suburbia, so there is a mixture of farmland, meadows and pastures, woodland, residential tracts, and the occasional campus of a school or corporate headquarters.

The five hundred-foot-high perspective from which you witness all this pleasant make-believe world is brand new. You are the beneficiary of an eye-transplant operation, the donor being an eagle.

As the moon influences the tides, so does the balloon you hang from cause life to change below you.

Dogs bark.

Youngsters pump their bicycles in hot pursuit.

Horses turn in their pens nervously.

Five deer burst from a soybean field where they have been browsing, scattering in all directions like a burst of fireworks.

Cows stare at you from over the bridge of their thick snouts. Until now you did not know cows had the wherewithal in their neck muscles to look up at anything. Cows look at their grass or their feed, or when bored with it all, they just look straight ahead with that lovely black blankness in their eyes. But to see cows look skyward—it shakes you up.

A woman hanging up laundry looks up and waves.

A man staking tomatoes in his garden straightens his old back and just looks.

Another man comes out on his front porch, shaving lather on half his face. He waves.

Below you the van of the chase crew moves along in your wake as best it can, its way continually blocked by dead-end streets, traffic lights, and unpaved countryside. The van disappears from time to time owing to these obstacles, but then reappears a bit later. If it were an animal, it would be out of breath trying to keep up with your shortcuts.

From time to time the pilot pulls on the blast valve, to keep the flight on an even keel, he says. "Novice pilots go up and down like Yo-Yos," he explains. "Ballooning is an art, not a science, and it takes time to develop the intuition you need to apply just the right amount of heat at just the right time."

It begins to rain lightly. Staring down at the earth through a soft rain is as mind boggling as watching a herd of cows stare up. If this is not an altered state of consciousness, you think, then nothing is.

"We're changing direction," the pilot announces. "Did you notice?"

You did not. The pilot shows you how it is possible to keep track of your

Landing: as the basket touches down, Bob pulls the rip line, opening the crown of the envelope and permitting air to escape rapidly. (Phil Smith)

position in relation to the earth by a trick of looking at the horizon line, and how by checking landmarks that you have passed from time to time can see whether you're on a straight or curving path.

You have diverged from the relatively straight line the balloon was on until now. You cross a ridge and then a long stretch of scrubland. You venture the guess that the chase crew is off the scent now for good.

"He'll find us," the pilot says. "And if he doesn't, we'll find each other—before taking off, you always decide on a phone number to call in case someone does get lost."

Off in the distance a 747 cuts through the air, sleek and soundless from where you are, and yet you think how envious the people on board would be if they could see you.

Another surprising disccovery: you have not been so relaxed in weeks. The ride has pulled the plug on your normal life, and your stress has gone down the drain.

COMING DOWN

Of course it has to end.

"We have to make a decision," says the pilot. "See those high-tension wires in the distance? Either we apply more heat and make sure we get well over those, and plan on landing somewhere on the other side of the next ridge, which will mean another half hour or so of flying time, or we pick a landing spot now. See that field in front of the brick house in the distance there, straight ahead? We could bring it in there."

You are prepared to stay up to cross another ridge or two—as many ridges as there is fuel for, actually—but then the chase crew might have more trouble catching up. It makes sense to end the flight here.

The pilot brings the balloon down in steps. At first you are not even aware you are descending, but that is part of the art. The pilot does not use the blast valve as often, and when he does, it is in shorter bursts.

But after crossing a line of trees, the balloon suddenly does appear to be quite low to the ground, and in fact on a crash course with the sloping yard in front of the old brick house looming ahead.

"I'm going to bring us down just a bit sooner because I don't want to hit that tree in the man's yard," the pilot says. The tree he is referring to is a scrawny weeping willow with no leafy growth on it that you can see, so you are impressed that the pilot could be so property-conscious at a moment like this.

Closer. The pilot has his hand on the red line that controls the deflation vent at the crown of the envelope. "Brace yourself by putting one foot up on the side of the basket and holding onto the rails of the basket with both hands, okay?" he says.

Pilot and passenger scamper out of the basket as surface wind helps blow the envelope to the ground. (Phil Smith)

Moments later the gondola meets the ground with a slight bump, tilts forward, then immediately rights itself. At the same time the pilot yanks down on the rope and the deflation port comes open. The hot air escapes at once. Above you the stately balloon dissolves into a cascade of brightly colored rags, falling forward of the craft and fainting dead away on the lawn.

AFTERMATH

At flight's end, inevitably, there is a slight feeling of disappointment, which a first-time flier named Barbara Jennings once described to a tee:

"My feet felt strangely heavy as I walked around our grounded gondola. I had that same weak-in-the-knees feeling you sometimes get after a long airplane ride, or like the astronauts must feel after orbiting the earth, or like when you've just fallen in love. The ground feels strange, foreign. I know it will pass, but somehow I don't want it to. I want to remain acclimated to the sky."

But there are still many things to be done and to be experienced, so you do not get a chance to brood for long about your premature return to earth.

The man who lives in the brick house near which you have landed comes running from his front door, still in the middle of tieing his necktie. "Where can I get one of those things?" he cries. "How can I get a ride in one?"

Bob and Vicki squeeze out the remaining air before packing up the balloon. (Phil Smith)

The pilot leaves off his postflight equipment check to deliver a polite nut-shell history of ballooning, and also to present the landowner with his card in case he really is serious about taking a ride some day.

After the pilot has made certain his burner system is properly shut down, he and Vicki stretch out the envelope. "The canvas bag is in the truck, so we'll have to wait for the chase crew to show up to do any packing," he says. He asks the landowner, "May I use your phone?"

"Sure, of course, come on in, all of you, come in! Would you like some coffee?"

The pilot places a call to the phone he and the chase crew have agreed upon to use to contact each other in advance. The chase crew has not phoned in yet, so the pilot leaves the number of the phone he is calling from.

Meanwhile, you have been wandering about still in a bit of a daze. Every once in a while you glance up at the sky in the direction you came down from. You are tempted to pinch yourself to be sure it all has happened as you believe it has. Yes, you have been flying in a balloon and seen cows look up at you and a flock of Canada geese fly beneath your basket. You decide that if you keep repeating things like that to yourself, eventually you will believe it really all did happen.

You follow the pilot and Vicki outside again. Coming up the driveway at a fast clip is the van of the chase crew. Hands and arms wave from windows on both sides. The crew are jubilant to have caught up with their prey unassisted by telecommunication.

After the chase crew arrives at the landing site, the celebration of the flight takes place. "May you fly so high and so well, God joins you in laughter." (Phil Smith)

"We lost you when you started drifting off to the west, over the ridge," says the driver as soon as he hops out of the van. "But we figured you'd come down somewhere along here. I'd say that was pretty good figuring!"

Someone else produces a bucket full of ice with a bottle of champagne in it, and glasses for all, including the landowner—who still hasn't finished tieing his necktie.

The pilot explains to you that it is customary to toast a person's first balloon voyage with champagne, and he pops the cork and fills the glasses. The landowner first refuses, saying he has to go to the office, then changes his mind. "The hell with it," he declares, beaming, taking the glass offered. "It's not every day this sort of thing happens to a man."

Everyone stands around sipping every ounce of pleasure out of the bubbles in his champagne. The pilot records the date of today's flight on the label on the champagne bottle, then signs his name. The landowner signs his name.

"What did you think?" says the pilot, handing the bottle over to you as a memento.

"It was great," you reply.

Not a Pulitzer Prize-winning statement by any means, but you really don't care. The rain has subsided here and given way to a morning full of light. Everyone in the circle of the celebration of your first aerial voyage seems happy for you and happy for himself. It is nine o'clock in the morning now, and the workaday world is swinging into life, but you have already lived your full day, and it is one you won't soon forget.

Your First Morning in the Sun 129

Chapter Ten

The Education of a Balloonist

What does it really take to become a balloonist?

There are a number of accredited balloon-pilot training schools in the United States and in Canada, which provide complete training programs. Obtaining a ballooning license, although it does not take very long, is not simple. Besides ten hours of in-flight training with one solo flight, applicants must also pass a written balloon-pilot's license exam, and be checked out by an FAA pilot examiner.

The specific requirements are spelled out by the FAA in their Federal Aviation Regulations (FARs).

Student pilots may begin training at age fourteen, and at age sixteen may earn a private license. A commercial license, enabling pilots to fly for compensation (such as taking on paying passengers or flying balloons for advertising or promotion purposes) requires more training. Applicants must pass a written exam covering the FARs, meteorology, and general rules about ballooning. They must take a check ride and demonstrate flight proficiency with an FAA examiner on board. Every two years, pilots must renew their ratings by passing a flight proficiency test known as the biennial flight review.

Some people decide to work toward a pilot's license after a fair amount of exposure to the sport, but most go into the sport promptly upon being bitten by the ballooning bug. Regardless of your entry, your subsequent "education" as an aeronaut can take many different forms. Indeed it should if you are to become well-rounded in your knowledge and proficiency.

The first thing you can do is go up for a ride. Pilots who are certified to carry passengers in their balloons are listed in Part Three and very likely there is at least one pilot within driving distance of your location. Most pilots charge from $50 to $100 for a ride averaging thirty minutes to one hour.

You can also volunteer to be part of a ground crew or chase crew for an established pilot. This will give you invaluble experience in all that goes into preparing for a flight, as well as what happens during and after the flight. The more you do this, the more you will know about the sport—and, chances are, the more friends you'll make in ballooning. You can contact individual pilots to offer your services, or you might contact one of the balloon clubs, also listed in Part Three.

To get thoroughly immersed in the atmosphere of the sport, you can attend ballooning rallies and races. The BFA sponsors its national balloon championship for hot air balloons every year, usually during the first week of August in Indianola, Iowa. The Albuquerque Balloon Fiesta is held during October and attracts upward of four hundred balloons from all over the world. It is the largest gathering of its kind in the world, and lasts several days. The International Professional Balloon Pilots Racing Association (I.P.B.) sponsors numerous races in and around major cities year-round, including the national professional ballooning championship. In addition to these events, many smaller events are conducted by local ballooning clubs and these sociable affairs can give you an interesting glimpse into the people who are into ballooning as well as the techniques involved in the activity.

There is no shortage of books about ballooning—the Library of Congress lists over six hundred titles. Many of these books are useful as well as highly entertaining, though the vast majority have to do with people and events associated with the early days of gas ballooning.

Another important and interesting source of information on the subject is *Ballooning*, a magazine published by the Balloon Federation of America. Appearing every other month, it features stories written by BFA members, innovations in the sport-balloon industry, technological and record-making feats in the lighter-than-air field, and the historic events, customs, and traditions of ballooning. In addition, it provides a limited schedule of balloon rallies and flying festivals, plus commercial advertising from manufacturers, pilot training schools, and individual traders. It really is must reading for the prospective pilot seeking more information and for sport flyers who wish to keep abreast of the latest developments.

If serious instruction in the sport is desired, enlist the services of a qualified teaching pilot. Training normally costs about $100–$150 per hour. Currently, a private license requires a *minimum* of ten hours' instruction, but virtually all authorities in the field urge prospective pilots to take more training to build up as much experience as possible. Training includes "ground school" time devoted to the scientific dynamics of balloon flight, FARs, balloon construction and component parts, and the study of wind and weather patterns as they affect the sport. In the field, on-site procedures are learned for rigging, inflating, and mooring the balloon and briefing crew members. Then maneuvers in the air are taught—various ascents and descents at controlled rates, maintaining level flight patterns for various distances, and landings in a variety of conditions.

The following chapters will not attempt to simulate an entire flight-training program, but rather will provide an overview of the types of skills and the range of knowledge covered. To give you an idea of the wide range of individual tasks and skills involved in learning to fly a balloon, we have outlined in Part Three the flight training program used at Sky Promotions in Princeton, New Jersey.

Chapter Eleven

The Anatomy of a Balloon

Basically, the hot air balloon consists of three parts: envelope, basket, and burner system. It's a fairly simple piece of equipment, and for what it delivers, it is something of a bargain.

If you look at what is available in flying machines, for instance, you may be surprised to find that ballooning is less than half as expensive as the next class of aircraft, the sailplane. Some recent studies have shown that the average price of a new hot air balloon system is about $9,000, but that of a sailplane is $22,000. A piston-driven single-engine airplane with fixed landing gear averages over $31,000, while the same type of plane with retractable gear costs over $64,000. Multiengine airplanes are three times this price, and helicopters are eight times this price. Turbo-engine aircraft range in the millions.

But relatively inexpensive as it is, the hot air balloon is a carefully conceived and crafted flying machine, and at this point it would be a good idea to explain more precisely what the components of this unusual flying vessel really are. Since there are differences in detail among the balloons made by the

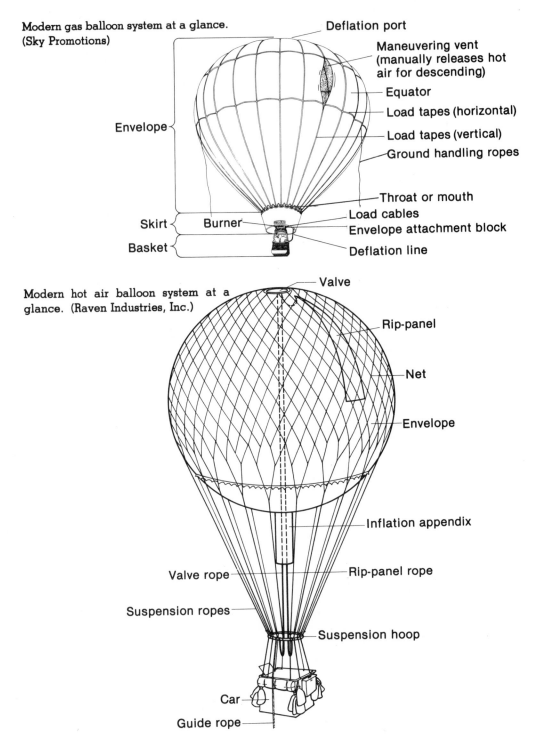

Modern gas balloon system at a glance. (Sky Promotions)

Deflation port

Maneuvering vent (manually releases hot air for descending)

Equator

Load tapes (horizontal)

Load tapes (vertical)

Ground handling ropes

Envelope

Throat or mouth

Load cables

Envelope attachment block

Deflation line

Skirt

Basket

Burner

Modern hot air balloon system at a glance. (Raven Industries, Inc.)

Valve

Rip-panel

Net

Envelope

Inflation appendix

Valve rope

Rip-panel rope

Suspension ropes

Suspension hoop

Car

Guide rope

various manufacturers, we will confine ourselves primarily to discussing the Raven S-55A, one of the most popular types and sizes of balloon in current use.

Balloons are categorized by the FAI (Fédération Aéronautique Internationale) according to how much air their envelopes can contain, much as sailboats are classified by length and/or sail configuration. The size classes and the average human cargo capacity for the classes in common use are given below:

Class	Volume (cubic feet)*	Capacity
AX–1	Up to 8828	
AX–2	8,829 – 14,124	
AX–3	14,125 – 21,186	
AX–4	21,187 – 31,780	1/2 – 1
AX–5	31,781 – 42,372	1
AX–6	42,373 – 56,496	1 – 2
* AX–7	56,497 – 77,682	2 – 3
AX–8	77,683 – 105,930	3 – 4
AX–9	105,931 – 141,240	5 – 8
AX–10	141,241 – 211,888	
AX–11	211,889 – 317,832	
AX–12	317,833 – 423,776	
AX–13	423,777 – 565,035	
AX–14	565,036 – 776,902	
AX–15	Over 776,923	

*The actual size categories are stated in cubic meters and these are the appropriate conversion numbers—hence, nonround figures.

The AX-1 balloon will not generally support an average-sized person, and the AX-2 or AX-3 will only lift a person if there is no attached gondola. The double-digit sizes—AX-10 and above—are not practical sport balloons due to their awesome size. We flew an AX-12 balloon called *Great Adventure* back in 1973 in connection with the opening of an amusement park of the same name in New Jersey. The envelope alone weighed eight hundred pounds. Just to inflate the balloon required an experienced eight-man crew and four blowers going for half an hour. It could carry as many as fourteen passengers, but like all large balloons the *Great Adventure* needed very calm wind conditions for launch and wide-open spaces for landings.

THE ENVELOPE

The part of the balloon that looks like a balloon is actually called an envelope, only it is one built to contain hot air instead of overdue bills or declarations of love. Some pilots also affectionately refer to it as "the bag." It is connected to the

Passenger capacity of balloons depends on envelope size. This early gas balloon, approximately 100,000 cubic feet capacity, could carry up to 30 passengers. (National Air and Space Museum, Smithsonian Institution)

The *Great Adventure*, at 400,000 cubic feet, one of the largest commercial hot air balloons ever constructed, could carry over 20 passengers. (Sky Promotions)

gondola, or basket, in which pilot and passengers ride, by means of stainless-steel suspension cables.

The fabric in the envelope is rip-stop, fire-resistant nylon, similar to material used in the backpacks or lightweight tents carried by hikers and mountaineers. It is woven in panels, two panels making up what is called a gore. There are twenty-four of these gores, or large vertical sections, in the entire S-55A envelope. The gores are held together by stitching and by heavy-duty load tapes—webbing similar to the material used in seat belts in automobiles—which help support the weight of the balloon and minimize strain on the fabric, thus prolonging the useful life of the vessel. The envelope is usually treated with a polyurethane coating to reduce porosity, and in the coating is an ultraviolet inhibitor to help the fabric withstand the rays of the sun.

The S-55A model, which measures fifty-five feet in diameter, has 1,075 yards of nylon in its envelope, or one fifth of an acre in surface area, more than three miles of thread, and almost half a mile of load tapes. Its 77,550-cubic-foot capacity translates as a space that could hold 62,279 bushels of apples, or, in liquid form, 579,940 gallons of apple juice.

The top cap or crown of the balloon may be designed in one of two ways. The standard top features a circular deflation port that is closed off by a circular panel, which is held sealed during flight by a flexible hook-and-loop closure. A deflation port line, usually called the rip line and colored red, extends from the

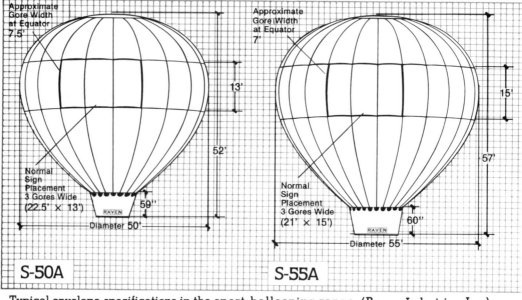

Approximate Gore Width at Equator 7.5'

Normal Sign Placement 3 Gores Wide (22.5' x 13')

RAVEN

13'

52'

59"

Diameter 50'

S-50A

Approximate Gore Width at Equator 7'

Normal Sign Placement 3 Gores Wide (21' x 15')

RAVEN

15'

57'

60"

Diameter 55'

S-55A

Typical envelope specifications in the sport-ballooning range. (Raven Industries, Inc.)

top to the basket and is pulled by the pilot upon landing to effect an almost instantaneous deflation of the envelope. Pull on the line, and the hook-and-loop closure comes open, and the hot air rushes out.

The parachute top also features an opening in the crown, along with a similar circular panel to fill the opening. In this case, the panel is rigged up with lines, as the name suggests, exactly like a parachute. It is used both for effecting a complete deflation of the envelope after landing, and also during flight to vent a limited amount of hot air as a means for controlling vertical ascent or descent. After landing in the parachute top balloon, the pilot pulls on the top line and holds it open for as long as he can until the envelope has been deflated.

Balloons built with the standard deflation port also feature an opening in the side known as the maneuvering vent, also initially sealed, like the deflation port, by hook-and-loop closure. This vent is operated by a rope called the maneuvering vent line, which extends from the vent to the basket. The pilot pulls the line, causing the side vent to open and allowing the hot air to escape to stop a rate of ascent or initiate a rate of descent. Once the line is released, the vent automatically recloses.

The venting/deflating system is one of the most important features in envelope design, and mastering the particular system involved is an important ingredient in becoming a competent balloonist. Before the advent of the modern

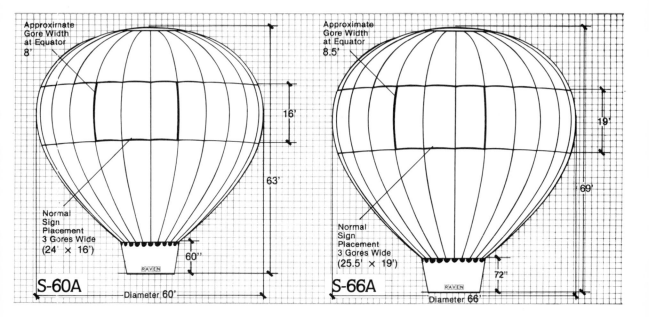

Approximate Gore Width at Equator 8'

Normal Sign Placement 3 Gores Wide (24' × 16')

16'

63'

60"

RAVEN

S-60A

Diameter 60'

Approximate Gore Width at Equator 8.5'

Normal Sign Placement 3 Gores Wide (25.5' × 19')

19'

69'

72'

RAVEN

S-66A

Diameter 66'

method for quick deflation, hapless pilots and their baskets were frequently dragged willy-nilly along the ground for many minutes before the flight could be terminated. Both during flight and upon landing, the venting/deflating system is essential to safe ballooning.

The envelope is equipped with three quarter-inch ground-handling lines. These lines are attached to the horizontal load tape circling the upper portion of the balloon and are held by crew members to keep the envelope in place during inflation or deflation, especially when these operations occur in windy conditions. Two shorter ground lines are attached to the throat of the envelope and are used by crew members to hold the balloon open during the inflation procedure.

A skirt is connected to the bottom section of the envelope with peelable tabs and helps create a stovepipe effect when the burner system is running, channeling the warm air into the balloon and improving fuel efficiency, especially on windy days, by protecting the burner from the wind.

Attached to the inside of the balloon envelope, near the top or crown, are temperature indicators known as telltales. These telltales are white when installed but turn black if the air in the envelope exceeds a certain temperature. This permits the pilot to tell at a glance when his balloon may need repair.

We mentioned earlier that the cubic capacity of an envelope dictates how many people can be carried aloft safely in a balloon. However, this capacity may be adjusted upward or downward depending on other factors, principally air temperature, altitude and what might be bluntly described as the Fatso Factor. The key is to determine the maximum safe gross weight that can be carried by the balloon on a given day. All balloons are provided with FAA-certified curves for estimating temperature-limited gross weight. These curves show gross weight in pounds versus air temperature in degrees Fahrenheit for operation at various pressure altitudes, usually sea level, 5,000, 10,000, and 15,000 feet MSL.

As an example, on a 70 degree day, an AX-7 can lift approximately 1,400 pounds at sea level, but only 1,200 pounds at 5,000 feet and only 1,000 pounds at 10,000 feet. If an AX-7 is rated at 1,434 pounds at sea level, its gross weight is distributed as follows: 170 pounds for the envelope, 290 pounds for empty basket (including instruments and empty tanks), 170 pounds for fuel, 72 pounds for extra equipment (helmets, tools, radios, drag rope, etc.), and 732 pounds for the allowable load of pilot and passengers. This implies that at sea level it can lift four 183-pound persons, one being the pilot in command. But in Denver, where the elevation is 5,000 feet, only three 183-pound persons can be carried aloft without exceeding the specified gross weight limit.

In the summertime, at Vail Pass in Colorado, where the elevation is 10,600, one more person would have to leave the basket. But in the wintertime, that person could get back in, and if the outside temperature dropped to 20 degrees Fahrenheit, all four persons could fly in the AX-7.

Bear in mind that four 183-pound persons are pushing the limit. It is likely that some of the people would weigh less than 183 pounds, and, in fact, the average weight could be below 150 pounds. It is advisable not to push to the limit, but instead take less weight than actually allowed. This will lower the envelope operating temperature and serve to increase envelope lifetime. Also, performance is more responsive at lower envelope temperatures.

THE BASKET

Currently, open-air passenger vessels for balloons are made either of wicker or aluminum and fiberglass. A rigid tubular framework extends from the basket upward where it attaches to the twenty-four stainless steel cables suspended from the envelope. This rigid framework actually serves three purposes: 1. it helps protect passengers; 2. it supports the burner system, which is installed overhead at the top of the basket; and 3. thanks to the mechanical-fulcrum effect, it provides the basket with stability and less of a tendency to tip over upon landing.

Baskets normally come in square or rectangular shapes. Triangular shapes also are available, and on special order one can obtain completely enclosed gondolas, or deluxe baskets with built-in banquette seats and insulated

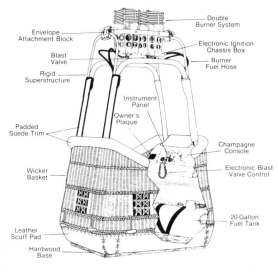

Labels on image:
Double Burner System
Envelope Attachment Block
Electronic Ignition Chassis Box
Blast Valve
Burner Fuel Hose
Rigid Superstructure
Instrument Panel
Owner's Plaque
Padded Suede Trim
Champagne Console
Wicker Basket
Electronic Blast Valve Control
20-Gallon Fuel Tank
Leather Scuff Pad
Hardwood Base

Typical basket, or gondola, with burner system in place. (Raven Industries, Inc.)

champagne holders. As a minimum, there must, of course, be room on board for securing the necessary fuel tanks and flight instruments. A typical basket for the AX-7 envelope, with full gear and fuel on board, may weigh over three hundred pounds.

Wicker is the classic or traditional look in a basket, but it is actually not just nostalgia that makes it a popular material, even though it costs more than aluminum-fiberglass varieties. The strong and resilient rattan that is woven around a tubular aluminum frame happens to provide an excellent shock absorber during less-than-perfect landings. The aluminum/fiberglass baskets are quite strong and lighter than wicker, and although they do not have as much "give" on impact, these baskets are often used for commercial ventures where more rugged conditions are the rule.

THE BURNER SYSTEM

If the envelope and the basket are the most visible parts of the balloon, our third major component, the burner system, is the motive force, for it produces the heated air which the pilot uses to lift off and to control his vessel's up-and-down motion once aloft.

In the AX-7 we're describing, there are one or two burners securely bolted to the uppermost frame of the basket (and also, through load blocks, to the suspension cables of the envelope), within easy reach of the pilot. One of the burners is usually gimballed, which simply means the pilot can swivel it at different angles, a handy feature during the inflation stage.

Normally the burner or burners point directly into the center of the

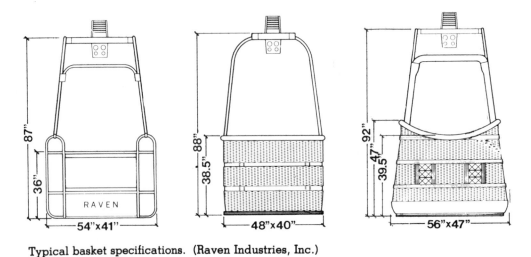

Typical basket specifications. (Raven Industries, Inc.)

balloon envelope. There is a pilot light very much like the kind found on ordinary gas stoves, and this assures rapid access to heat whenever necessary. There is also a blast valve allowing the pilot to adjust the rate at which fuel flows from the tanks. To draw fuel into the burner, the pilot simply pulls the trigger on his blast valve. The liquid propane gas is carried under pressure from the fuel tank to the burner, where it is set on fire by the pilot light. A pressure gauge on the burner tells what this pressure is. The propane is transferred from tanks in the basket through flexible hose to the burner system. The fuel goes through coils on the burner which vaporize the liquid gas. Then the pilot light ignites the vapor, sending a six- to eight-foot flame into the envelope, making a loud whooshing sound and adding heat at the rate of 12 million Btu's per hour.

The Btu is defined as the quantity of heat required to raise the temperature of one pound of water by one degree Fahrenheit. To give a better idea of the tremendous output of a burner system in a hot air balloon, one burner produces at a rate per hour that would be enough to heat 120 three-bedroom homes comfortably. Propane, the fuel used almost exclusively in hot air ballooning, has the additional advantage of being readily available and quite inexpensive in today's energy-scarce world. Also called liquefied petroleum gas, or LPG, it is a by-product of the petroleum-manufacturing process. A typical hour-long flight in an AX-7 would consume ten-twelve gallons of propane, costing in today's market under $20 total. Propane is odorless, incidentally, so as a safety measure refineries introduced an ingredient called mercaptan into the gas. Mercaptan has a strong, sweetish scent, which makes gas leaks readily detectable.

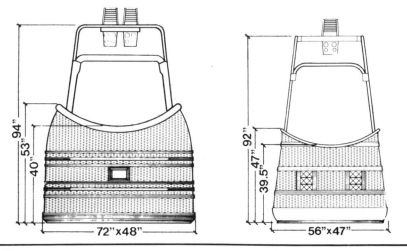

The propane is stored in fuel tanks, either ten-gallon aluminum or twenty-gallon stainless-steel tanks. The advantage of the more expensive stainless-steel tank is that it is lighter, so you can carry more fuel with less tank weight. On a typical flight, you would carry a minimum of three ten-gallon aluminum tanks or two twenty-gallon stainless-steel tanks. Both types of tanks come equipped with fuel indicator gauges. Experienced pilots consult these gauges but also double-check their readings by keeping track of fuel consumption in terms of the amount of time they have been flying.

There are two ways of heating air inside the envelope. One is by triggering the blast valve, as mentioned, which when wide open can add heat at the rate of 12 million Btu's per hour. Intermittent blasts during flight enable the pilot to maintain a standard temperature in the balloon, and a standard temperature generally provides a standard altitude for that flight.

The second method of adding heat to the envelope is by using the "cruise" or metering valve. By monitoring the exact flow of propane to the burner, you can then maintain a steady output from the burner, which will provide a standard temperature. This would enable you to maintain a straight and level flight without having to touch the blast valve that often. It's as close as you can come to flying on automatic pilot in a hot air balloon.

There are three reasons often cited for including a second burner in a burner system.

First and foremost, the second burner provides a safety factor known in the aviation industry as "redundancy." As on a two-engine plane, if one engine

Close-up of burners and basket frame.
(Raven Industries, Inc.)

fails, the pilot still can get back to earth safely, so in the hot air balloon a pilot can maintain much more control over his destiny if he has a back-up burner to call upon if need be.

The second reason is that twice as much firepower is available. This provides more heat instantaneously in case it is needed.

Finally, there is a psychological advantage in having the second burner on board. Generally, the more relaxed and confident a balloonist is, the better he flies.

Some commercial balloons, incidentally, are equipped with special single burners for superpressure operations, where certain modifications are used so that the burner can be used for both free and tethered flight.

OTHER BALLOONING GEAR

We've covered the three basic components of the hot air balloon—envelope, basket, and burner system—but there are other items of equipment that pilots need and sometimes use frequently. Some of these items are required (by the FAA), some simply recommended out of common sense, and some that might be described as optional in the same sense that mud flaps and FM radios are optional on new cars. Let's look at them briefly before moving on to the actual process of inflating a balloon for flight.

REQUIRED

Altimeter. This tells you how high you are above the ground, normally giving readings in feet above sea level, and can be adjusted to the local ground elevation where the ascent is taking place.

Variometer. This is basically a rate-of-climb meter and lets you know first of all if you are moving up or down. That may sound ridiculous, but at altitudes of 1,000 feet or more, where visual references are few and far between, it is often quite difficult to judge such basic facts of life as whether you are on the way up, or on the way down. The variometer also measures the vertical speed of the balloon in feet per minute or second.

Pyrometer. An electrical sensor installed near the top or crown of the envelope sends information to this meter in the basket. It tells the temperature of the air in that area. As with RPM's in an automobile, there is a "red line" not to exceed in terms of envelope temperature, beyond which you risk damaging fabric strength. The pyrometer helps you monitor this important factor.

Fuel gauge. This shows how much propane is left in the tanks on board, and because fuel supply is important to a safe and sane balloon flight, such gauges should be as reliable and visible as possible.

Sparker. This gadget comes in handy for quickly reigniting a pilot light that has inadvertently gone out. Most pilots carry two sparkers—plus a cigarette lighter and a pack of dry matches, to be on the safe side. Sparkers are also used by welders and by campers for starting up Coleman lanterns, so they are readily available.

Headgear. Protective hats or helmets are vital safeguards in the event of a fast or bouncy landing. As with lifeboats on a ship, there should be enough on board for all occupants.

Flight Manual.

RECOMMENDED

Protective Clothing. There is no point in totally ignoring the remote but real chances for injury involved in ballooning. In that spirit, let's note a few simple precautions to incorporate in your standard garb for the sport.

The pilot should wear some eye-protecting device—goggles or simply a pair of sunglasses—during the inflation stage. This will shield his eyes from any backlash of heat from an unexpected gust of wind blowing flames from the burner toward him instead of toward the envelope, and conceivably save a nice set of eyebrows.

Pilot and crew should wear heavy-duty gloves as protection from the heat of the burner and its flames, and also from possible rope burns.

Pilot and crew should wear long-sleeved shirts and long pants, again to protect themselves from the heat and flame of the burner system during inflation—cotton or fire-retardant materials are preferred, not nylon and polyester.

Pilot, crew, and passengers should wear sturdy boots or high shoes so everyone is more comfortable in the rough or slippery terrain one might conceivably land in.

Fire Extinguisher. It should be of the type useful in combating propane-fueled fires, and carried not only in the chase vehicle but on board balloon. The super 10 ABC is the type often recommended.

First Aid Kit. It should include silver compound medication for burns and, like the fire extinguisher, be carried both on board and in the chase vehicle.

Balloon Log Book. The pilot records the date, place, and other pertinent details of every one of his flights in the given balloon.

Pilot Log Book. Pilot logs appropriate flying hours in appropriate balloon.

OPTIONAL

Electric Blast Valve. This is a push-button valve control that can be operated from anywhere in the basket.

Electronic Ignition. Similar to above, this operates off a battery and keeps the pilot light going.

Compass. Until recently, FAA regulations required that balloonists carry a magnetic compass on board, but this device plays no practical role, at least not on short flights. On long flights in unfamiliar country, it does give you an idea of the exact direction in which you are gradually getting lost.

Communication System. On short flights there is no particular need to be in touch with Houston Control. Aviation radios and transponders are useful on board for long flights at high altitudes, and radios are in fact required to be carried if you are flying through any airport traffic control zone. The CB radio may be a convenient tool for staying in touch with your ground crew, but beware of its potential role as a distraction. If you're talking good-buddy talk on the CB and taking your mind off flying, you are likely to wind up in a tall tree.

Safety Line. Or drag rope or drop line. This is a rope, usually about a hundred feet long, that is coiled like a ball of yarn in the basket and sometimes thrown to members of the crew, at the end of a flight, to help in bringing the balloon under control more quickly. We have listed it as optional equipment because the drag rope is potentially quite dangerous. It can snag on fences or power lines, for one thing. Also, the person at the other end, if ignorant of ballooning, could suffer rope burns or be dragged with the line into unforgivingly hard obstacles, like tree trunks.

Chapter Twelve

Inflation of the Balloon

It takes about half an hour to set up and inflate an AX-7 balloon for flight. Here are the steps involved.

SELECTION OF THE LAUNCH SITE

Actually, experienced pilots often select *several* potential launch sites for a given flight and don't make a final choice until they are reasonably sure the direction of the wind will provide a pleasant flight. One's usual goal is to leave from a site and be able to float over the most picturesque or interesting terrain available in the area.

The site itself should be in an open, grassy area, easy to get to and a safe distance from obstructions such as power lines, and out of the controlled air zones surrounding airports and defense facilities. It is also a good idea to set up a reasonable distance from any residences or farm animals in the area, as the noise of the burner system could be disturbing and distracting, particularly in the predawn period when many balloonists prefer to launch.

CHECK OF THE WEATHER

Prior to any planned launch, the balloonist usually contacts the local FAA flight service station, for information such as the current weather report, forecasted weather, and surface winds, storms that may be moving into the area, cloud ceilings, visibility, and winds aloft. The winds aloft provide readings in wind speed and direction at 3,000-foot increments, and are worth checking because they often give an indication of potential surface winds.

Weather information should be checked and rechecked, for it can change drastically in twelve hours or less. Many balloonists make it a practice to brief themselves on the weather the night before a planned launch, then first thing in the morning before departing for the launch site, and finally just prior to launch, in order to be sure they are going up in the favorable weather conditions they expect. As one pilot once astutely noted, "It is better to be down here wishing you were up there than up there wishing you were down here."

Most pilots and crews find that takeoffs and landings go more smoothly when surface winds are no more than eight or ten knots (a knot equals 1.151 miles per hour). As one becomes more experienced, it is possible to go up in higher winds safely.

In theory, the balloonist can take off, travel a distance, rise to a new altitude where the wind is going in the direction of his launch site, and so execute a perfect round trip. Days such as this, though, are few and far between.

Cloudy skies are sometimes an advantage as the clouds reduce the heat-up of the earth and slow down the wind development. They can stretch good flying weather into the late morning hours for an early launch, or can retard the development of adverse winds such as thermals.

BRIEFING OF THE CREW

Crew members are usually recruited several days in advance of a launch so that the pilot is certain he will have enough personnel on hand at the launch site at the right time. Although some sports balloonists have devised ingenious methods for inflating their balloons unassisted or with the aid of only one or two other people, the recommended standard procedure is that at least two or three able-bodied assistants be on hand to help with the inflation and the chase.

At the launch site, once it has been determined that conditions are appropriate for flying, the fun begins. The crew is briefed as to duties and responsibilities. The basket and balloon bag containing the envelope are unloaded from the van or pickup. The envelope is pulled out and stretched along the ground and attached to the basket and burner system. Suspension cables are sorted out and hooked into position. Fuel lines are attended to and checked for leaks, and as a precaution, the basket is secured to the chase vehicle with a rope.

The deflation port in the crown of the envelope and the maneuvering vent on the side are both checked to be sure they are properly sealed.

INFLATION OF THE ENVELOPE

Now the greatest labor-saving device since sliced bread is wheeled out. This is no more than a large fan powered by a gas engine. It simply blows air into the envelope. Before it came on the scene, people got a balloon partially inflated by holding it at the throat and flapping up and down to coax air inside. This resulted in enormous biceps and long waits.

The fan is set up a few feet from the throat or neck of the balloon, then started. Crew members hold the envelope open at the throat and the pilot directs the air blowing inside the balloon. This inflation procedure takes only about ten minutes. While it is going on, the pilot walks around his balloon as it gradually takes shape on the ground and checks for any tangled lines, holes in the fabric, etc. He then walks inside the balloon to check temperature telltales and the general condition of the fabric, and to make sure the vent line and rip line are not snarled and that the top cap is secure.

HEATING THE AIR IN THE ENVELOPE

After his inspection tour, the pilot returns to the basket, again checks for leaks in the burner system, makes sure all necessary instrument and other gear are on board, and spells out the final preflight procedures for the crew. He then ignites the pilot light and turns on the blast valve, directing the flame directly into the envelope. The balloon quivers with life as hot air pushes against the fabric. The pilot keeps the burners on as the balloon slowly fills and rises from the ground, pulling the basket with the pilot inside upright as it reaches near buoyancy.

Just prior to equilibrium—the moment at which the buoyancy of the balloon overcomes gravity—the pilot makes final preflight checks, boards any passengers, and gives final instructions to the crew. Then the pilot checks both upwind and downwind to be sure his course is still obstacle-free and he makes sure crew members and onlookers are in the clear. Lift-off is accomplished by one or more short blasts of hot air.

Contrary to popular belief, a balloon does not take off straight up, soaring into space. The balloon lifts itself a few inches above the ground and moves slowly away at an angle, depending on the speed of the wind and the amount of heat in the balloon.

Chapter Thirteen

The Art of Ballooning

It is often said that flying a balloon is more of an art than a science, and in many respects this is true. That is why newcomers to ballooning, even though they may be highly experienced in other forms of aviation, require time and training to get the knack of handling an aerostat—the technical name for a balloon.

But though flying is an art, it takes several different types of awareness, each composed of an observable phenomenon and common-sense understanding of the instruments themselves, in order to become proficient and to get the most out of the game. And this means making use of what science has to offer.

Let's look at the five major categories of awareness and explain the role each plays in the successful flight of the balloon.

AWARENESS OF THE AEROSTAT

This means getting to know intimately the gentle-looking giant you are flying: "Know thy balloon." This really starts when you first sign on as a crew member, at which time the pilot will explain what you are to expect—or as much as he feels you need to know and can absorb. But the real challenge comes when you are aloft in the balloon and must plug into its nervous system.

A good comparison would be to the different feeling you have driving

153

your own car and driving a rental car that is strange to you. You know instinctively how your car should sound, drive, and react, and as a result you can operate it more safely and effectively in a variety of conditions. With a rental car you are much less in tune with its automotive properties and probably not as good a motorist in it as you are in your own vehicle.

In terms of ballooning, knowing what you have to do with the burner system, in order to clear a tree line and then land a balloon in a short field on the other side, is the same kind of instinctive driving knowledge you have developed for passing other cars or rounding curves.

The first thing one learns as a student pilot is when to turn up the burner to gain height. There is invariably a delayed response of ten to fifteen seconds or more between the time heat is applied and the time the large craft, with its two tons of heated air, responds. This is called anticipatory flying. Beginners characteristically fly in a Yo-Yo pattern through the air, up and down, the result of applying heat too late and too long, then of waiting too long again before the next blast. The excess heat sends the balloon into a rapidly rising ascent. Then the excess cooling sends it plummeting again.

The experienced pilot, by contrast, uses anticipatory flying to move along at a steady altitude. When he does make an ascent or a descent, he does so as on an invisible staircase, almost with a sixth sense, stepping up and stepping down, as the case may be, with periods of level movement in between. By tethering the balloon in calm wind conditions, the newcomer can more easily get a feeling for the balloon's response to heat.

Use of the maneuvering vent is an equally important subtlety of craft awareness. The effect of venting varies according to the length of time the vent is held open but also according to balloon temperature and atmosphere conditions. In your own automobile, you know exactly when to apply the brakes to prevent yourself from tailgating. In the balloon, the experienced pilot develops a similar instinct for what effect venting will have on the flight.

Craft awareness also means sensitivity to the instruments on board, using them to confirm or deny your own observations. In warmer weather, for instance, it's a good idea to keep a close watch on the pyrometer as the envelope temperature is more likely to exceed tolerable limits.

Craft awareness includes constant attention to the burner system and the fuel supply. There is only so much flying time in each propane tank, and the wise pilot does not go solely by the gauges on the tanks themselves, but also by his own reckoning as to how long he can safely stay aloft.

AWARENESS OF THE ATMOSPHERE

This means knowing as much as humanly possible about the wind and weather conditions in which you are flying, and being constantly on the lookout for signs that these conditions are changing—which is the rule rather than the exception in ballooning.

This category includes meteorological savvy—recognizing your basic cloud formations, knowing your cold fronts and warm fronts and stationary fronts, and above all understanding the year-long wind-and-weather patterns in your own area. The good balloonist becomes as familiar with his local weather conditions as does the successful farmer or gardener.

Don Piccard has noted:

"The true greatness in a balloon lies in its basic simplicity in design and function balanced against the unending variations of the environment and its reactions to these changing circumstances."

Since many environmental variations are invisible, one could add to that statement that the true greatness of the balloonist lies in his ability to read them.

Atmosphere awareness, then, includes simple things like observing changes in speed or direction, and noting, for example, a sudden feeling of air rushing against your face during flight—an indication of moving from one layer of air into another with probable changes of effect on the flight.

While practical experience in this regard is essential, atmosphere awareness can be increased by a certain amount of book learning. One book highly recommended by a former chairman of the BFA Safety Committee is *Meteorology for Glider Pilots*, by C. E. Wallington, (London) John Murray. Even more than balloonists, glider pilots depend on knowledge of wind and weather to function, and this book clearly presents a large amount of information on a complex subject. Another book of great interest and value is *Fires*, published by the U.S. Department of Interior. Intended primarily as an aid to understanding and controlling forest fires, it nevertheless contains a wealth of good information on the behavior of the wind in various circumstances.

To provide a glimpse into the true complexity of atmosphere awareness, let us look closely at just one aspect of the weather of tremendous importance to balloonists—summer thunderstorms and thermals.

At 12,000 to 16,000 feet, small cumulus clouds of summer flourish and grow rapidly to large towering (20,000 to 60,000 feet) cumulonimbus thunderstorm clouds. Surprisingly, an afternoon thermal, or small orographic disturbance, can trigger the development of a thunderstorm by initiating the rise of warm moist air. Most severe thunderstorm development occurs along or just ahead of summer cold fronts. They materialize in a squall line several hundred miles long at times. Invariably, there is a continuous line of strong gusty winds, violent updrafts of several thousand feet per minute, wind-shear turbulence, thunder roll, lightning strokes, hail, heavy rainfall, and even flash floods. Some of the more ferocious storms also spawn tornadoes. Obviously, these are not conditions suitable for balloon flying.

It should be noted that much is still unknown about just how thunderstorms operate. For instance, scientists still do not fully understand what causes lightning and its close association with rain. Some think lightning serves as a catalyst in the formation of rain while others believe that the rapid descent of charged rain or hail generates lightning.

Here in the United States, winds gusting to sixty and seventy MPH are often observed, usually moving from west to east or from northeast to southeast. Radar studies show the thunderstorm life cycle, from start of growth through maturity to dissipation, to be very short and somewhat complex. It is difficult to forecast and communicate short-term storm details to remote locations—often the locations where ballooning takes place. By the very nature of the storm's behavior, one area may be missed while another may experience high winds and a torrential downpour. This is why balloonists must keep a watchful eye for a rapidly darkening western or southwestern sky followed by distant thunder and lightning, as well as local irregular shifts in wind speed and direction. Such symptoms provide approximately thirty minutes of advance warning. Dust on the horizon signals the onset of gusty surface winds of the encroaching storm center. Upper wind direction can be determined by observing the direction of the anvil-shaped cloud blowing out ahead of the system.

Peak gusts of a raging thunderstorm strike abruptly and leave little time for a safe landing. Even airplanes have broken up in flight several miles from a storm, so one can just imagine what could happen to a relatively frail balloon.

A thunderstorm is said to reach maturity when rain begins to fall. Since the storm is essentially vertical, the falling rain penetrates the clouds and its aerodynamic drag creates downdrafts. Each drop causes more drops to precipitate, and so more air is dragged downward. The result is a mass of down-rushing air that turns at right angles when it reaches the surface and then spreads out away from the column of heavy precipitation. Most of the down-rushing air turns in.the direction of the overall storm movement, creating a gust front that could cause a lot of excitement for the unwary balloon pilot.

Even though thunderheads may be seen forming in the distance, the balloonist can easily be tempted to continue flying in gentle surface winds. However, cumulonimbus clouds can affect wind currents as far away as ten miles with abrupt changes. The balloon can actually be drawn into the storm center as warm moist air flows inward toward the rising vertical columns of air. It is therefore highly advisable never to venture closer than ten miles. Instead, land and terminate all ballooning activity for the day.

Summertime is also thermal season, and it would be wise for all balloonists to respect the sun-generated weather phenomenon known as the thermal. When the lower atmosphere is heated and the lapse rate of air becomes dry-adiabatic, the conditions are ideal for triggering thermal development.

Surfaces with low solar reflectivity and with shelter from the wind are the most likely breeding grounds. Calm conditions promote thermals by allowing more time for isolated or sheltered pockets of air to be solar-heated. Here, more heat energy is provided than the surface can absorb. The extra heat is transferred to the air by convection, causing it to become buoyant. As the bubble of superheated air rises, it displaces the air above it, forcing it into an unstable condition. Under these conditions, as thermals form, a balloon's drift may be abruptly shifted in speed and direction without a change in altitude or it may begin to trace a wide curved path. These are the first signs of thermal activity. Southeast-facing slopes have greater potential for thermal development than flat terrain, because of the higher sun angles, thus permitting more solar heating. Thermals, like balloons, tend to drift with the wind (so one may ride along with it for a while), but break up when the wind speed exceeds fifteen to twenty knots.

As in the case of the thunderstorm, a balloon can be drawn into the center of a thermal, where the action of the vortex can cause the basket to swing outward beneath the envelope as the balloon traces a spiraling path that climbs at an alarming rate, perhaps more than 1,000 FPM. This is false climb, since no heat was added to the envelope by the burners. The pilot must anticipate a sudden loss of lift and a potential downdraft when the balloon pops out of the thermal. Heat should be applied to offset a rapid uncontrolled descent. The flattening and distorting stresses on the top panel could cause an inadvertent rip out at high altitude or the side panels could split open. For this reason, the first sign of thermal activity should herald the end of ballooning for that day.

In the summer months, the sun rises earlier and heats the ground sooner. Sun angles are high, and therefore the morning flight hours are reduced, especially when the air is clear, dry, and calm. Fortunately, weak thermals precede more powerful thermals. The unstable conditions during early thermal development normally warn the pilot of the impending danger, but only if he is alert to subtle changes in his balloon's behavior.

AWARENESS OF THE LAND

You have to know the sky to fly a balloon, and you also have to know what the ground is telling you.

This means, first and foremost, knowing what's on the ground below the balloon throughout the entire flight. Needless accidents can occur when inexperienced pilots fail to take the simple precaution of standing in the basket and facing in the direction they are flying in, or talk on the CB instead of watching where they are going.

Through experience, you will learn a whole bag of tricks of seeing—using the horizon line and other perspective references for example—to tell if you are rising or falling, whether you are on a steady or curving course, where a descent at any time is likely to bring your balloon down, and so on.

Awareness of the land also interacts with atmosphere awareness, in that terrain characteristics can have a profound effect on wind conditions. Whether you are flying over mountains, through mountain valleys, or over bodies of water, the balloon reacts in certain predictable, and sometimes unpredictable, ways, and it is the pilot's job to anticipate such reactions as best he can. Those who consistently fly in the foothills of the Rockies learn what the wind currents will be at various hours of the day during the year. Those who fly over the wheat fields of Kansas know precisely when thermal activity will begin. Those who fly in congested suburban areas become adept at landing on a dime. Those who fly in the desert learn the subtleties of flying by night.

AWARENESS OF OTHER PEOPLE

This is part of the art of flying, because the success of any flight depends so much on other people, and the safety and comfort of other people depends so much on the pilot.

It starts with the acquisition of weather information from the forecasters, with whom the pilot must establish a thoroughly professional relationship.

It continues with the ground crew and chase crew. The pilot must be responsible in his thinking and clear in his instructions throughout the preparations for flying, making sure every member of the crew knows his or her job, and constantly being aware of their safety.

In flight, people awareness obviously continues with any passengers on board and most importantly as landing nears.

People awareness also has to do with people on the ground who have nothing to do with the flight per se. Their tranquillity and the safety of their pets and farm animals should always be on the pilot's mind. Getting high enough—at least five hundred feet—when passing over farm country and barnyards is a must, because chickens, ducks, pigs, and horses can be terror struck by a balloon.

Waving from the balloon or calling hello as you pass overhead goes a long way toward diminishing the possibly irritating early-morning noise of the burners—only the coldest personality fails to wave back.

People and the property they own or live on must be on the pilot's mind in selecting a landing site. It is better to touch down in a plowed field or a meadow than in a front lawn or a field with crops growing in it. For the sake of the chase crew, it also makes sense to find a landing area that is reasonably close to a road or highway.

People awareness in ballooning really boils down to the compassion and consideration preached by the Golden Rule—do unto others as you would have aeronauts do unto you.

SELF-AWARENESS

The fifth and final category of awareness essential to ballooning is simply self-awareness. The pilot must know himself like the back of his hand—actual skills and qualifications, not imagined ones, and actual experience in various different conditions of flight.

The pilot must be confident of his own ability, but wary of developing a self-image inflated with hot air. Toward this end, he should occasionally remind himself that the people on the ground are looking up at the balloon, not at him.

A healthy respect for one's limitations will obligate him to develop something all pilots in every form of aviation use, and that is the checklist. This is the perfect foil for such human foibles as forgetfulness and momentary distraction. A checklist should be consulted for every significant phase of ballooning, including preflight activities, inflation, prelaunch activities, lift-off, landing, and postlanding activities. Detailed sample checklists are reproduced in Part Three.

Not long ago Ed Yost, the father of modern hot air ballooning, offered these five suggestions for safe flying, and we reprint them here from *Ballooning Journal*, because they, too, depend on self-awareness:

1. Fly only good safe equipment. You are issued only one life so why not defer the ending of it as long as possible?
2. Learn from the best qualified instructor available. The student usually flies like his teacher so find the best.
3. For the first twenty hours, fly in open fields and under light wind conditions. As you gain in proficiency, confidence, and experience, then move to more hostile terrain and increased wind velocities.
4. Be careful! Don't get talked into flying when common sense tells you to stay on the ground. Exhibition flights before a crowd of people present an excellent opportunity to get clobbered.
5. It's easy to make a reputation, but hell to live up to it.

Chapter Fourteen

Getting Started in Ballooning

If you think you might like to try ballooning, it is not as difficult to get started as you may believe.

The first step is to take a ride. We have listed in Part Three numerous balloon clubs and the leading balloon manufacturers in this country, any of whom can recommend a qualified pilot in your area. Ballooning, like any other sport, has its rip-off artists and ne'er-do-wells, so it is important to obtain good references to be sure your first ride is a representative and enjoyable one.

Once you have gone for your ride, you'll know whether or not you've got balloon fever. If you do, your next step will be training.

Again, look for a reputable flight instructor, usually found within the structure of a reputable company. Be sure the teacher holds a commercial pilot certificate with a lighter-than-air free balloon rating. Select an experienced instructor, and check with other balloonists on his reputation for safety and competence. You can also contact your local FAA office to find out the instructor's safety record and reputation with aviation authorities in the area. Currently, you only need a minimum of ten hours of instruction for your private license, but regulations will probably increase this minimum in the near future.

A basic training syllabus describing ground school and balloon flight maneuvers can be found in Part Three and will give you a concrete idea of the kind of things that must be learned in order to qualify for a balloon pilot license.

Is training expensive? Costs vary from around $100 to $150 per hour for topflight instruction. Since you will need a minimum of ten hours, that means it could cost you up to $1,500 for training. In the aviation field that's a bargain—it costs much more to qualify as a pilot of fixed-wing aircraft.

What's next? Why, a balloon, of course. What has to be done to get one of those?

In Part Three we have listed major manufacturers of balloon systems in this country, along with the names of their dealers and distributors nationwide. Take the time to send for the free literature each manufacturer makes available for potential customers, and carefully compare the products that are available. Decide on the balloon you want, basing your choice on the use you plan to make of it. Sport ballooning and commercial ballooning are two different aspects of the game and usually do necessitate a difference in choice of equipment.

The cost of the balloon itself will vary according to how elaborate you want it to be. Used balloons can be purchased for as little as $5,000, while larger ones run as high as $10,000 to $25,000 if equipped with electronic navigational aids and other optional equipment. Generally speaking, though, costs for a brand-new balloon complete with all that is needed to fly will run about $8,000 to $9,000—about what it would cost you for a boat or a second car, and quite a bit less than for a small airplane.

Hot air ballooning is very inexpensive once the balloon is purchased. Propane gas costs about $20 for two hours of flying. Gas ballooning is quite expensive, since the helium can only be used once. To fill a gas balloon with helium costs about $3,000 per flight.

There is a shortcut to balloon ownership that numerous balloonists have employed. This is to form a group or club of three or four, or as many as five or ten, interested individuals, pool your resources and amortize the costs among you. This way you could get your license to fly in your club balloon for a commitment of not much more than $500 a year. Most good balloons, with standard maintenance, proper care, and no overheating or undue exposure to the sun, will last for many years.

If you do decide to check out second-hand balloons, make sure you have the manufacturer test the fabric of the envelope you are planning to buy. It is very hard to tell from cursory inspection whether or not a balloon has been misused or overheated.

Above all, become well informed before you make any move in ballooning. Opinions and emotions tend to vary sharply in this burgeoning new field, and your only defense as a consumer is the facts. To get them, you must write to and talk to as many pilots, organizations, and companies as you can. Make up your mind about instruction or purchase of equipment only after you feel comfortable with all the facts that you can gather.

Chapter Fifteen

Code of Ballooning and Etiquette for Aeronauts

COMMON SENSE AND SAFETY

1. Don't take off in any wind you would not want to land in.
2. Use checklists for every phase of every operation.
3. Always look in the direction you are traveling.
4. If you have any doubts about flying on a particular day—any questions or concerns at all about the suitability of wind and weather conditions—don't go.
5. Don't fly over populated areas in the early morning hours.
6. Always try to land downwind of power lines or other obstacles.

LANDOWNER RELATIONS

1. Always be respectful, courteous, and friendly.
2. Try to ask for permission to land before settling your balloon down.
3. Pick a landing site that will create the least possible inconvenience to the farmer or homeowner. In the case of farm property, pick a field free of crops and be particularly careful of animals on the approach.
4. After landing, discourage onlookers from coming into the property unless the landowner is present and has given permission.
5. Always get permission before bringing a chase vehicle onto someone's property.
6. Make sure that fences and gates are left as you found them when you landed.
7. Don't let anyone litter the area where you land.
8. If damage is caused and the landowner wishes to take further action, calmly exchange names and addresses in anticipation of an amicable settlement.

Part Three
The Balloonist's Baedeker

Official FAA Requirements—Balloon Pilot's License

The following information is extracted and simplified from Federal Aviation Regulation Part 61—Certification: Pilots and Flight Instructors.

A student pilot's certificate must be obtained before beginning training. Successful completion of training leads to a private pilot's certificate, lighter-than-air category with a free balloon class rating. After further training and experience a commercial rating may be obtained, qualifying an individual to fly for hire or to instruct. The following are the general requirements for student, private, and commercial certificates.

SUBPART C—STUDENT PILOTS

1. A student must be at least fourteen years of age.
2. He must be able to read, speak, and understand the English language (some exceptions allowed).
3. No medical certificate is required, but the applicant must certify that he has no known medical defect that makes him unable to pilot a free balloon.
4. Student pilot certificates may be issued by FAA inspectors or designated pilot examiners.
5. Student pilots may solo after demonstrating to their instructor that they are familiar with Part 91 of the Federal Aviation Regulations and are proficient in the following aspects of balloon operation: preflight preparation, operation of controls, lift-off and climb, descent and landing, and emergency situations.
6. A student pilot may fly a balloon only under the supervision of a qualified instructor. He may not carry passengers or fly a balloon for hire.

SUBPART D—PRIVATE PILOTS

1. To be eligible for a free balloon private pilot's certificate a person must be at least sixteen years of age.
2. Read, speak, and understand the English language.
3. No medical certificate required. Same as paragraph 3 above.
4. The applicant must pass a written test on such items as (a) Federal Aviation Regulations covering pilot privileges, limitations, and flight procedures, (b) use of navigation charts, (c) recognition of weather conditions and use of weather reports, (d) operating procedures with gas and hot air balloons.

5. The applicant must have received instruction on the following pilot operations: (a) ground handling and inflation, (b) preflight checks, (c) takeoff and ascents, (d) descents and landings, (e) emergency conditions.

6. Flight experience must include at least 10 hours in free balloons, which must include six flights under the supervision of an instructor. These flights must include at least the following: two flights of at least thirty minutes duration, one ascent to 3,000 feet above takeoff point, and one solo flight (these requirements are for hot air balloons; requirements for gas balloons are slightly different).

SUBPART E–COMMERCIAL PILOTS

1. The age requirement for a commercial pilot certificate is eighteen years.
2. Read, speak, and understand the English language.
3. No medical certificate required. Same as paragraph 3 above.
4. The applicant must pass a more advanced written test on the subject matter listed in paragraph 4 above, additional operating procedures relating to commercial operations, and those duties required of a flight instructor.
5. Advanced training must be received from an authorized instructor including those items listed in paragraph 5 above plus emergency recovery from a terminal velocity descent.
6. The applicant for a commercial certificate must have at least thirty-five hours of flight time as a pilot, of which twenty hours must be in balloons (remaining fifteen hours may be in other aircraft). Flight time must include ten flights in free balloons, six under the supervision of an instructor, two solo flights, two flights of at least one hour duration, and one flight to 5,000 feet above the takeoff point.
7. The holder of a commercial pilot's certificate may operate a balloon for hire and may give flight instruction.

Ballooning Training Syllabus

Based on the curriculum used at Sky Promotions, Princeton, New Jersey.

GROUND SCHOOL

FLIGHT MANEUVERS

CHECKLISTS

GROUND SCHOOL LESSON 1, PRINCIPLES OF FLIGHT

Objective:

To provide the student with the basic knowledge of physics necessary to understand the principles of balloon flight.

Duration:

1.0 hours, individual instruction.

Description:

(A) Lift
1. Properties of gases
2. Atmospheric effects on gases
3. Hot air and gas balloon comparisons
(B) False lift
(C) Heat
1. Measures
2. Sources
(D) Propane
(E) Butane

Acceptable Performance:

Demonstrate adequate knowledge by attaining a minimum grade of 70 percent on an examination of the subject material.

GROUND SCHOOL LESSON 2, METEOROLOGY

Objective:

To provide the student with knowledge of weather recognition and forecasts necessary to the conduct of safe balloon flight.

Duration:

4.0 hours, individual instruction.

Description:

(A) Weather Theory
1. Basic atmospheric circulation
2. Air masses
3. Cloud formation and types
4. Elements of weather and effects
5. Fronts and thunderstorms
(B) Weather report and forecasts
1. Weather services
2. Hourly reports
3. Forecasts
4. Notams
5. Sigmets, Airmets, and Pireps
(C) Weather charts
1. Surface analysis charts
2. Weather depiction charts
3. Weather prognosis charts

Acceptable Performance:

Demonstrate adequate knowledge by attaining a minimum grade of 70 percent on an examination of the subject material.

GROUND SCHOOL LESSON 3, NAVIGATION

Objective:

To provide the student with the navigational skills and knowledge of airspace limitations necessary for the safe and lawful balloon flight.

Duration:

3.0 hours, individual instruction.

Description:

(A) Flight computer
(B) Sectional and WAC charts
(C) Dead reckoning
(D) Control areas and zones
(E) Flight planning

Acceptable Performance:

Demonstrate adequate knowledge by attaining a minimum grade of 70 percent on an examination of the subject material.

GROUND TRAINING LESSON 4, REGULATIONS

Objective:

To acquaint the student with the appropriate regulations governing balloon flight.

Duration:

1.0 hours, individual instruction.

Description:

(A) Federal aviation regulations
  1. Part 1
  2. Part 31
  3. Part 61
  4. Part 71
  5. Part 91
  6. Part 101
(B) US SIR
  1. Part 430
(C) Airman's information manual

Acceptable Performance:

Demonstrate adequate knowledge by attaining a minimum grade of 70 percent on an examination of the subject material.

GROUND TRAINING LESSON 5, FLIGHT HANDBOOK

Objective:

To familiarize the student with all the information available in the flight manual, with emphasis on knowledge of the limitations.

Duration:

1.0 hours, individual instruction.

Description:

(A) Limitations
(B) Normal procedures
  1. Preflight
  2. Flight
  3. Landing
(C) Emergency procedures
  1. Overtemperature
  2. Burner relight
(D) Performance
(E) Specifications
(F) Equipment list

Acceptable performance:

Demonstrate adequate knowledge by attaining a minimum grade of 70 percent on an examination of the subject material.

GROUND TRAINING LESSON 6.
FLIGHT MANEUVERS
AND TECHNIQUES

Objective:

To provide the student with the knowledge of the maneuvers and techniques that will be used in the flight training section of this curriculum.

Duration:

5.0 hours, individual instruction.

Description:

(A) Maneuvers
1. Preflight
2. Inflation
3. Prelift-off
4. Instrument references
5. Visual references
6. Burner system
7. Maneuvering vent
8. Inflation port
9. Fuel management
10. Lift-off
11. Climb with blast valve
12. Climb with cruise valve
13. Transition from climb to level flight using blast valve
14. Transition from climb to level flight using cruise valve
15. Level flight using blast or cruise valve
16. Descent with blast valve
17. Descent with cruise valve
18. Transition from descent to level flight with blast valve
19. Transition from descent to level flight using cruise valve
20. Terminal velocity descent
21. Approach to landing
22. Aborting approaches and descents
23. Aborting climbs
24. Landing
25. Postlanding
26. Emergencies

(B) Techniques
1. Blast valve
2. Aids to visual references
3. Vent timing
4. Control delay
5. Deflation port timing
6. Recognition of false lift
7. Recognition of thermal action
8. Detection of fuel pressure drop
9. Detection of flame out
10. Cruise valve control
11. Relights
12. Obstacles
    (a) recognition
    (b) avoidance
    (c) wires
13. Up and down drafts
    (a) detection
    (b) avoidance
    (c) combating
14. Ground handling ropes
15. Tether lines
16. Drag line
17. Deflation

Acceptable Performance:

Demonstrate adequate knowledge by attaining a minimum grade of 70 percent on an examination of the subject material.

GROUND TRAINING LESSON 7, ENGINEERING

Objective:

To thoroughly acquaint the student with equipment being used for flight training within this curriculum.

Duration:

2.0 hours, individual instruction.

Description:

(A) Basket
1. Construction
2. Assembly and disassembly
3. Inspection
(B) Burner system
1. Pilot light
   (a) construction
   (b) operation
2. Cruise valve
   (a) construction
   (b) operation
3. Blast valve
   (a) construction
   (b) operation
4. Pressure regulator
   (a) construction
   (b) operation
5. Care and storage
(C) Envelope
1. Construction
   (a) Basic envelope
   (b) Deflation port
   (c) Maneuvering vent
   (d) Skirt
   (e) Telltales
2. Care and storage
   (a) Normal

(b) Hazards
(c) Repairs
(D) Fuel system
1. Tanks
   (a) Construction
   (b) Gauges
   (c) Operation
   (d) Care and Storage
2. Lines and Fittings
   (a) Construction
   (b) Operation
   (c) Care and storage
(E) Instruments
1. Mounting and dismounting panel
2. Pyrometer
   (a) Construction
   (b) Operation
3. Variometer
   (a) Construction
   (b) Operation
4. Altimeter
   (a) Construction
   (b) Operation
5. Compass
   (a) Construction
   (b) Operation
6. Care and storage
(F) Inflation fan
1. Construction
2. Operation
3. Care and storage

Acceptable Performance

Demonstrate adequate knowledge by attaining a minimum grade of 70 percent on an examination of the subject material.

GROUND TRAINING LESSON 8, GROUND CREWS

Objective:

To provide the student with the knowledge to select, instruct, and use a ground crew safely and efficiently.

Duration:

1.0 hours, individual instruction.

Description:

(A) Throat
1. Protective clothing
2. Position
3. Duties
4. Safety precautions
(B) Crown line
1. Protective clothing
2. Position
3. Duties
4. Safety precautions
(C) Inflation assistants
1. Protective clothing
2. Position
3. Duties
4. Safety precautions
(D) Lift-off crew
1. Protective clothing
2. Position
3. Duties
4. Safety precautions

Acceptable Performance:

Demonstrate adequate knowledge by attaining a minimum grade of 70 percent on an examination of the subject material.

GROUND TRAINING LESSON 9, SAFETY

Objective:

To emphasize the areas of balloon flight which present hazards, and the methods and knowledge necessary to avoid these hazards.

Duration:

1.0 hours, individual instruction.

Description:

(A) Ground
1. Equipment
2. Crew members
3. Spectators
4. Launch-site selection
5. Deflation
6. Weather briefing and assessment
(B) Airborne
1. Power lines
2. Thermals
3. Drag line
4. Protective clothing
5. Weather avoidance
6. Passenger briefing
7. Trees
8. Icing
9. Flameouts
10. Landing personal safety
11. Emergency procedures
(C) Medical facts
1. Oxygen needs
2. Vertigo and vision
3. Motion drugs and alcohol effects
4. Psychological considerations

Acceptable Performance:

Demonstrate adequate knowledge by attaining a minimum grade of 70 percent on an examination of the subject material.

FLIGHT LESSON MANEUVER DESCRIPTIONS INDEX

Preflight

(A) Fuel
    1. Check quantity (normal training flights will start with all tanks filled to capacity).
    2. Install tank-checking security.
    3. Clear fuel lines.
    4. Connect and test fuel system for leaks
(B) Burner system operational check
    1. Pilot valve.
    2. Cruise valve.
    3. Blast valve.
(C) Loading
    1. Determine gross weight.
    2. Determine altitude limitation.
(D) Check deflation port closed.
(E) Check temperature telltales.
(F) Check maneuvering vent sealed.
(G) Instruments checked and secured.
    1. Altimeter
    2. Variometer
    3. Pyrometer
    4. Compass
(H) Drag line aboard and secured.
(I) Igniters (2 minimum) checked and aboard.
(J) Check inflation fan operation.

Inflation

(A) Position basket for proper fuel feed.
(B) Spread envelope out properly.
(C) Assign and brief ground crew.
(D) Perform cold inflation.
(E) Envelope check.
    1. Fabric integrity.
    2. Deflation port strap clear.
    3. Maneuvering vent line clear.
    4. Recheck deflation port and maneuver vent sealed.
(F) Use burner to inflate to upright position.
(G) Aborting inflation.
    1. Open deflation port with rip line.
    2. Maintain crew positions until envelope completely deflates.
    3. To reinflate, return to Step A of inflation.

Prelift-Off

(A) Secure maneuvering vent line and deflation port strap to basket.
(B) Re-check fabric integrity, vent, and port.
(C) Fuel selection.
    1. Draw fuel from each source.
    2. Select fullest tank.
    3. Insure tank valves are either full-on or full-off.
(D) Adjust pilot light and cruise valve as needed.
(E) Instruments
    1. Set altimeter.
    2. Turn on variometer and set to O.
    3. Check pyrometer operation.
(F) Set pressure regulator.
(G) Check ground handling lines and tether ropes free.
(H) Recheck minimum of two functioning igniters aboard.
(I) Protective head gear for all occupants.

Instrument References

(A) Pyrometer
    1. Always note reading at initial equilibrium before lift-off.
        (a) To determine if safe climb out can be achieved without overheating.
        (b) To provide a temperature reference during flight.
    2. Use readings to forecast changes in altitude.
    3. Cross-check readings to determine if changes in altitude are the result of heat input or atmospheric action.
    4. It is a secondary instrument reference.
(B) Variometer
    1. It is extremely important to activate the instrument and set it to O prior to lift-off. Otherwise, no accurate reference point can be established when airborne.
    2. Sensitivity varies and adjustments in references are necessary to achieve proficient use.
    3. It is the primary instrument reference.
(C) Altimeter
    1. It should be set prior to lift-off.
    2. Lag is to be anticipated.
    3. It is a secondary instrument reference.

Visual References

(A) Always position yourself to face in the direction of movement to insure the sighting of obstacles in your flight path.
(B) The visual reference is the absolute primary reference, and instrument references are also used to build proficient visual flight references.
(C) Altitude variations are best perceived by sighting toward a point 20 degrees below the horizon. This should also be done 90 degrees to the direction of travel so that drift movement does not confuse the reading.
(D) During descent for landing, visually locate a point on the ground that is neither moving nor below your line of sight. Determine your projected point of touchdown.

Burner System

(A) Use of pilot light
    1. The pilot light should be on at all times.
    2. The pilot light can be lighted or relighted, using the cruise valve.
(B) Use of the cruise valve
    1. To light it—
        (a) Turn it completely off.
        (b) Place sparker in proximity of nozzle opening.

(c) Crack valve slightly (only enough to produce about a 6-inch to 10-inch flame).

2. To relight pilot light, repeat lighting steps, and if this is not sufficient, slowly increase flame until pilot light ignition occurs.

3. To use as substitute for, or supplement to pilot light, follow lighting steps and adjust flame to level that will stay lighted. The cooling of the valve caused by restricted flow will cause temperature reduction. This will necessitate frequent adjustment and possibly cause freeze-up if blast valve is not used frequently. This is not a good alternative for routine use. It usually causes excess sooting.

4. Normal use
   (a) Regulate valve to produce desired continuous heat.
   (b) Readjustments are frequently needed and constant monitoring of pyrometer is required to maintain desired performance, especially when changing altitude.
   (c) Monitor ice formation to prevent freeze-up and use blast valve to clear ice as needed.

(C) Use of blast valve

1. Always determine that a fire source is available in the way of the pilot light or cruise valve before pulling the blast valve.

2. Always check for balloon material to clear the blast flame area before using.

3. Never partially open the blast valve (except during inflation). When used, it is full-on or full-off.

4. Desired envelope temperature is maintained by varying the length of blast time and/or the interval between blasts.

5. As a general rule, the more accurate altitude control, especially near the ground, will result from using frequent short blasts.

6. During the lift-off it is important to provide for a short interval within the first few feet of ascent. This will allow you to hear any warnings shouted by ground crew members of conditions of which you are unaware (i.e. ground line fouled, crew member or other person still holding on to basket).

Use of the Maneuvering Vent

(A) The vent is used to release hot air and reduce total lift of the balloon.

(B) Desired loss of lift is provided by varying the size of the opening and/or the length of time held open.

(C) Generally it is easier to achieve proficiency by consistently using the same size opening and varying the time.

(D) After the first use, the vent may not fully close and a small amount of air may continually escape. This will necessitate a compensation with burner input. All vents on the newer manufactured balloons close completely.

(E) The vent will have lag in effectiveness, as does the burner. In general, this lag will be shorter and the effects more pronounced.

(F) The vent is used to initiate a descent more rapidly than normal cooling, and must be compensated for with application of heat to prevent excessive rate of descent. This is more critical at low level.

(G) When releasing the vent line, visually check that the vent has returned to the normal position.

(H) Use of the vent increases fuel consumption.

(I) Use of the vent may initiate a rotation about the vertical axis.

Use of the Deflation Port

(A) The rip line for opening should only be used to deflate the balloon on the ground.

(B) Extreme care must be taken to prevent any opening of the deflation port prior to landing.

(C) When opened, it should be done rapidly and sufficiently to prevent ground travel.

(D) After opening, no further attempts should be made to reheat the envelope.
Emergency Considerations
   (1) Top should be opened prior to touchdown in high-wind landings.
   (2) Top should be opened prior to touchdown if there could be an imminent power-line contact by not opening it.

Fuel Management

(A) Except in special circumstances, all fuel tanks on board will be filled to capacity.

(B) All tanks on board will be connected to the burner system, whereby no connecting or disconnecting is required while airborne.

(C) Prior to lift-off, fuel will be drawn from each tank to insure availability from each source.

(D) Each tank will be depleted to 20 percent capacity and held in reserve for landing.

(E) Tank valves will always be turned full on or off to preclude freeze-ups.

(F) Empty unconnected tanks will be kept closed to prevent moisture contamination.

Lift-off

Normal
(A) Obtain equilibrium.
(B) Check and note pyrometer reading.
(C) Check that ground crew and spectators are clear.
(D) Using blast valve, proceed with lift-off with sufficient rate of climb to clear all obstacles (initial rate of heating should be high to insure safe lift-off with regard to possible false lift and wind shift or increase in velocity).
(E) Monitor pyrometer and variometer.
With Positive Buoyancy (to overcome obstacles or compensate for high wind or false lift)

(A) Use the same steps as in normal lift-off with the following additional steps between steps C and D:
   1. Brief two ground crew members only to hold the balloon down while additional heat over that required for equilibrium is applied (normally 20 degress F additional will suffice).
   2. On a predetermined positive signal from the pilot, the ground crew members will simultaneously release the balloon.

Climb With Blast Valve

(A) Start with constant altitude of at least 1,000 feet AGL (above ground level).
(B) Use heat to establish rate of ascent.
(C) Progressively increase rate of ascent one FPM for each foot of altitude gained.
(D) At 500 feet above initial altitude, a rate-of ascent of 500 FPM will be achieved.
(E) Maintain a 500 FPM ascent for climb.

Climb With Cruise Valve

(A) Start with constant altitude of at least 1,000 feet AGL.
(B) Use heat to establish rate of ascent.
(C) Progressively increase rate of ascent 1.5 FPM for each foot of altitude gained.
(D) At 750 feet above initial altitude, a rate-of ascent of 500 FPM will be achieved.
(E) Maintain a 500 FPM ascent for climb.

Transition From Climb to Level Flight Using Blast Valve

(A) Start from a 500 FPM ascent rate.
(B) Diminish heat supply to reduce rate of ascent beginning 500 feet below desired altitude.
(C) Progressively reduce rate of ascent one FPM for each foot of altitude gained.
(D) Stabilize balloon in level flight at desired altitude.

Transition From Climb to Level Flight Using Cruise Valve

(A) Start from a 500 FPM ascent rate.
(B) Diminish heat supply to reduce rate of ascent beginning 750 feet below desired altitude.
(C) Progressively reduce rate of ascent 1.5 FPM for each foot of altitude.
(D) Stabilize balloon in level flight at desired altitude.

Level Flight Using Blast Valve or Cruise Valve

(A) Apply heat to maintain desired altitude.
(B) Make corrections using the methods described for transition from ascents and descents making progressively slower rates.

Descent With Blast Valve

(A) Start at level flight at least 1,500 feet AGL.
(B) Reduce heat to establish descent.
(C) Progressively increase rate of descent one FPM for each one foot descended.
(D) At 500 feet below initial altitude, a rate of descent of 500 FPM will be established.
(E) Maintain a 500 FPM rate of descent.

Descent With Cruise Valve

(A) Start at level flight at least 200 feet AGL.
(B) Reduce heat to establish descent.
(C) Progressively increase rate of descent one FPM for each 1.5 feet descended.
(D) At 750 feet below initial altitude, a rate of descent of 500 FPM will be established.
(E) Maintain a 500 FPM rate of descent.

Transition From Descent to Level Flight Using Blast Valve

(A) Start at a 500 FPM descent.
(B) 500 feet above desired altitude, use heat to initiate a slower rate of descent.
(C) Progressively reduce rate of descent one FPM for each one foot descended.
(D) Stabilize balloon in level flight at desired altitude.

Transition From Descent to Level Flight Using Cruise Valve

(A) Start at a 500 FPM descent.
(B) 750 feet above desired altitude, use heat to initiate a slower rate of descent.
(C) Progressively reduce rate of descent one FPM for each 1.5 feet descended.
(D) Stabilize balloon in level flight at desired altitude.

Terminal Velocity Descent

(A) Start in level flight at least 5,000 feet AGL.
(B) Turn up cruise valve enough to maintain flame source during descent.
(C) Allow envelope to cool and descend, progressing to terminal rate.
(D) Use blast valve to prevent freeze-up of cruise valve during descent.
(E) Monitor throat area to observe possible caving in.
(F) Adjust pressure regulator (if any).
(G) At a minimum of 2,000 feet AGL (note altitude) use blast valve steadily until a rate of descent is reduced to 300 FPM; thereafter continue to use blast valve as needed to level off with a minimum loss of altitude.

Approach to Landing

(A) Preparation
1. Stow all loose gear.
2. Prepare drag line for easy deployment.
3. Adjust cruise valve to provide alternate pilot light function.
4. Use blast valve only to regulate heat.
5. Rely on visual references during approach.
6. Check that fuel supply selection is sufficient to complete approach and regain sufficient altitude if approach is aborted.
(B) Normal approach
1. Establish a rate of descent that will safely clear all obstacles and provide for a direct line-of-sight movement toward intended landing area.
2. Maintain the relative position of the intended landing area throughout the approach.
3. Do not establish a rate of descent in excess of the balloon's altitude AGL (i.e. AGL altitude 200 feet—maximum rate of descent 200 FPM).
4. Properly executed, the use of the maneuvering vent should not be necessary although it is not excluded.
(C) Steep approach using the maneuvering vent (to clear high obstacles, land in small areas, etc.)
1. Establish level flight at the lowest safe altitude possible as the intended landing area draws near.
2. As the final obstacle is being cleared, fully open the maneuvering vent for an interval that will initiate the descent, yet allow time for recovering with reheating.
3. Reheat the envelope promptly to control touchdown rate of descent.

Aborting Approaches and Descents

(A) Use blast valve only.
(B) Apply heat with blast valve until descent is checked and climb is initiated.
(C) Recover to level flight at desired altitude.

Aborting Climbs

(A) Open maneuvering vent till ascent is checked and descent is initiated.
(B) Recover from descent at desired altitude with blast valve.

Landing

(A) Preparation
1. Position occupants side-by-side, facing the direction of movement, using up-wind structures for hand holds.
2. Burners off prior to touchdown, release grip on burner controls, leave fuel tank valve and pilot light on.
3. Flex knees and cushion landing impact with legs.
(B) Touchdown in light winds
1. Just prior to touchdown, open maneuvering vent, holding it open until ground travel ceases.
(C) Touchdown in high winds and/or with limited ground travel clearances
1. Simultaneously with touchdown, open deflation port as quickly as possible to its maximum.
2. Hold it from reclosing until ground travel has ceased, or longer if necessary.
(D) Water landings
1. In light winds, proceed with normal landing techniques and keep balloon inflated, if possible.
2. In high winds:

(a) Position occupants so that they can exit to the side.

(b) After impact, move all occupants outside.

(c) Maintain position outside of basket, remaining with balloon; the basket will float and provide buoyancy.

(E) Posttouchdown

1. Remain in the basket, keeping all parts of the body within the confines of it.

2. Stay as low as possible.

3. Remain clear of burners, fuel lines, and fittings.

4. Except in necessary emergencies, do not exit until it is determined that the balloon will remain stable while you do so.

Postlanding

(A) Turn off fuel tanks and purge fuel lines.

(B) Turn off variometer.

(C) Reseal maneuvering vent and deflation port.

(D) Inspect envelope and basket for damage.

(E) Stow envelope.

Emergency Procedures

(A) Burner and fuel system
1. Pilot light
2. Cruise valve
3. Blast valve
4. Tank valve
5. Valve icing
6. Fuel leaks

(B) Instruments
1. Pyrometer
2. Altimeter
3. Variometer

(C) Controls
1. Maneuvering vent
2. Deflation port

(D) Overtemperature

(E) Engine inoperative

(F) Landings with high rate of descent

CHECKLIST

Before Starting

1. Fuel quantity / *Checked*
2. Fuel system / *Tested and secure*
3. Burner system / *Tested and off*
4. Loading / *Within limits*
5. Deflation port / *Sealed*
6. Maneuvering vent / *Sealed*
7. Temperature telltales / *Checked*
8. Fabric, lines, and cables / *Inspected*
9. Basket / *Checked and positioned*
10. Envelope / *Positioned*
11. All lines and straps / *Free and positioned*
12. Instruments / *Installed*
13. Drag line / *Aboard*
14. Igniters / *Two aboard*
15. Inflation fan / *Check*
16. Ground crew / *Briefed and assigned*

Before Takeoff

1. Deflation port strap / *Secured and accessible*
2. Maneuvering vent line / *Secured and accessible*
3. Envelope and basket integrity / *Checked*
4. Pilot light and cruise valve / *Adjusted*
5. Altimeter / *Set*
6. Variometer / *On and set to 0*
7. Pressure regulator / *Set*
8. Handling lines / *Free*
9. Igniters / *Two aboard*
10. Protective clothing / *As needed by occupants*
11. Passengers and flight crew / *Briefed*
12. Fuel / *On fullest tank*

Cruise

1. Fuel management / *Monitored*

Before Landing

1. Loose gear / *Stowed*
2. Drag line / *Positioned for deployment*
3. Pilot light and cruise valve / *Adjusted*
4. Fuel / *Check ample quantity to complete landing*
5. Passengers / *Positioned and briefed*

After Landing

1. Fuel / *Off*
2. Variometer / *Off*

Stopping Engine

1. Cruise valve / *Partially open*
2. Fuel lines / *Purged until flame is extinguished*
3. All valves, except pilot valve / *Off*

EMERGENCY CHECK LIST — EMERGENCY OPERATION OF FUEL SYSTEM

Malfunction

1. Pilot light out

2. Pilot light will not re-light

3. Blast valve or cruise valve will not open

4. Blast valve or cruise valve will not close

5. Icing of blast or cruise valve

6. Tank valve will not open

Corrective Action

Relight with striker. If it will not light, crack cruise valve and light it, turn up cruise valve until pilot lights.

Cycle valve. If no response, use cruise valve as substitute pilot light (monitor icing of cruise valve).

If unresponsive to hand pressure, use wrench on valve stem retaining nut to loosen one-half turn (never remove), re-attempt hand opening. If successful or unsuccessful, *retighten retaining nut* sufficiently to prevent leakage. *Never* apply wrench leverage to valve handle. Land as soon as practical.

Repeat action for cruise valve not opening. If valve is open to the degree that envelope temperature cannot be stabilized below a controllable point (below maximum temperature or continuous climb rate), use fuel tank valve to control output and maneuvering vent to control ascent. Land as soon as practical.

Turn valve off and use opposite valve until radiant heat of burner eliminates ice. If unable to move valve and controllability is affected, use procedures for Number 3 above.

If unable to open using hand pressure, *do not use wrench*. Switch to other tank and land as soon as practical.

7.	Tank valve will not close	If unable to close using hand pressure, *do not use wrench*. Be aware that no backup exists for blast or cruise valve sticking on. Land as soon as practical. After landing, use caution handling fuel system until condition can be corrected.
8.	Icing of tank valve	Open valve fully or close fully, using alternate tank. If valve sticks, use procedures for those malfunctions.
9.	Rupture of fuel line or valve	Turn off all tanks and follow procedures for burner inoperative procedure, Emergency Operation number 8.
10.	Fuel leaks	Tighten where possible with wrench. *Avoid excessive force*. If uncorrectable, land as soon as practical.

EMERGENCY OPERATION OF INSTRUMENTS AND CONTROLS

1.	Pyrometer failure	Disconnect wire, check for contact failure, reconnect. Tap gauge with hand. Use slow rates of ascent and descent in maneuvering to a landing as soon as practical.
2.	Altimeter failure	Use visual references and variometer reference as alternate.
3.	Variometer failure	Use visual references and altimeter reference as alternate.
4.	Maneuvering vent will not open	Adjust maneuvering with heat input to preclude using vent.
5.	Maneuvering vent will not close	Use additional heat to compensate for loss and land as soon as practical.
6.	Deflation port will not open	Use maneuvering vent as alternate.
7.	Deflation port opens in flight	Compensate for loss of heat with increased use of burner. Land as soon as possible. If unable to maintain altitude, continue to use maximum burner output and follow procedures for burner inoperative.

8. Burner inoperative

When reoperation is impossible, turn off all tank valves and purge fuel system; jettison all possible weight, considering safety of persons and property on the ground. Secure all remaining items. *Use maneuvering vent only to avoid extreme hazards (power lines, etc.) or to substantially improve touchdown area (e.g. to land in trees or terrain that will cushion touchdown).*

EMERGENCY CHECK LIST — PERSONAL SAFETY FOR TOUCHDOWN AT HIGH RATE OF DESCENT

1. Put on all clothing available.
2. Remove eyeglasses, if unnecessary.
3. Position occupants where each has as much space to move as possible without interference.
4. Remain upright with knees flexed and allow yourself to collapse to the bottom of the basket upon touchdown.
5. If landing in trees, remain as low as possible within the basket.
6. As a general rule, remain in the basket until all movement ceases. (Other hazards such as fire or potential fire could override this.)

EXCESSIVE ENVELOPE TEMPERATURE

1. Descend to minimum practical altitude.
2. Continue flight with minimum practical vertical maneuvering.
3. If envelope temperature is not reduced to acceptable level by above action, land as soon as practical and investigate cause.

Ballooning Organizations

Fédération Aéronautique Internationale
6, rue Galiley
75016 Paris
France

The Fédération Aéronautique Internationale (FAI), headquartered in Paris, is the world authority for official certification of aviation record achievements. It was organized in 1903 and comprises forty-seven member nations plus twenty associate members. As such, it sanctions all world sport aviation championships.

The first aviation record was established by Alberto Santos-Dumont of Brazil in 1906 with a speed of 41.292 KPH. Since that time FAI record activity has grown to include almost every aspect of aviation. The latest edition of the official records book has twenty different categories, many with several classes in each category. Over the years the FAI has grown and expanded its scope of operations. It sponsors all world sport aviation championships, undertakes continuous modernization of the Sporting Code which permits fair and scientific comparison of the performance attained by pilots of different nations, facilitates international air travel by noncommercial aircraft, evaluates aeronautical progress through the organization of international meetings and granting of medals and diplomas, and is the international body that groups together the National Aero Clubs of member countries. Each FAI member country is required to have an Aero Club. In the United States it is the National Aeronautic Association.

National Aeronautic Association
821 15th Street, N.W., Suite 430
Washington, D.C. 20005

The National Aeronautic Association (NAA) is the oldest, most prestigious, independent, nonprofit aviation organization in the United States. With a history dating back to 1905, the NAA is the sole United States representative to the FAI and as such is the only organi-

zation in our country that can sanction and certify official national and world aviation record flights. It represents the interests of more than 150,000 sport aviation enthusiasts, who make up the membership of NAA's divisions and affiliates. The NAA is headquartered in Washington, D.C.

The NAA was chartered in 1922 as the successor to the Aero Club of America, which was founded by balloonists in 1905. Prior to the passing of the Aeronautics Act of 1926, the NAA issued all pilot licenses in the United States. Today it issues all FAI Aviation Sporting Licenses for pilots. As the United States representative to the FAI, the NAA occupies an important seat at the international aviation conference table, participating in the establishment of sound and equitable rules and procedures for safety and equality in world aviation events.

The five primary purposes of the NAA are as follows:

1. Keep the public informed of the importance of aviation and space flight to the national security, economic progress, and international understanding.
2. Call for sound national programs designed to keep the United States first in aviation and space flight.
3. Support a vigorous aviation and space education program for students at all levels of learning.
4. Encourage, sanction, aid, and document sporting and record-making aviation and space events in accordance with the rules prescribed by the FAI.
5. Recognize and honor those who make outstanding contributions to the advancement of aviation and space flight and related subjects.

The NAA has a large board of directors, a long list of corporate members, fourteen divisions, and many chapters. The Balloon Federation of America is a division of the

NAA. On March 26, 1961, Francis Shields and Peter Pellegrino met with NAA and National LTA Society representatives to organize the BFA as a division of the NAA for the promotion of ties between aeronauts in the United States and the rest of the world. Up to that time, the Balloon Club of America had been functioning as the sole viable vehicle in matters of free ballooning in this country. In 1967, Ed Yost, Don Kersten, and Peter Pellegrino met at the NAA in Washington and rewrote the constitution to bring it in line with the new era of hot air ballooning.

Internationally, the BFA represents the United States on the FAI's international sport balloon committee at its annual meeting in Paris. This committee is called Comité Internationale d'Aérostation (CIA).

Balloon Federation of America
Suite 430, 821 15th Street N.W.
Washington, D.C. 20005

The Balloon Federation of America (BFA) was founded in 1961 as a division of the National Aeronautic Association (NAA) to advance the sport of ballooning and to promote ties between aeronauts in the United States and the rest of the world. At the end of 1980 the BFA had approximately 3,500 members, of which 2,100 hold a private or commercial balloon license. Almost all of the active pilots who hold altitude, distance, or duration records are members of the BFA.

The BFA, through the NAA, is the sole representative for American balloonists to the world governing body for sport aviation, the Fédération Aéronautique Internationale (FAI).

The BFA opens channels of communications for pilots and interested nonpilots. The regular publications of the BFA are *Ballooning*, published bimonthly and mailed to all members, *The Pilot Newsletter*, published monthly and mailed to all licensed balloon pilot members, *Welcome to the Balloon Federation of America*, a booklet describing many aspects of aerostation, and an *Events Guidelines Manual*. An annual roster of pilot members is also produced and is available to BFA pilot members.

The BFA does not itself organize any events other than the BFA National Championships. However, the BFA does sanction balloon rallies when certain criteria are met. The present BFA Events Policy was inaugurated in August 1974 at the United States Nationals by a vote of the general membership. Prior to that time, open participation in the Nationals competition had been a fairly simple matter, considering that from 1970 through 1973, there were fewer than 100 competitors registered. By 1974, however, with 150 pilots actually taking part, it was obvious that at the projected growth rate, the logistics of continued open competition would create astronomical problems. The need to establish a fair method of evaluating pilot skills to determine entrants in the Nationals competition automatically created a mandate for the BFA to develop a Nationals ranking system. In the autumn of 1974, the Events Committee was authorized by the board of directors to produce the present BFA National Ranking System. It became operable in January of 1975 and offered criteria for the selection of those pilots who competed for the title of BFA National Air Balloon Champion in that year.

The BFA National Championships are the culmination of a year of balloon competitions and rallies. Each year, aeronauts gather at the Nationals to exchange stories, to demonstrate new techniques or equipment, to participate in the Annual BFA General Membership meeting, and to determine the top pilots in the United States who will be the representatives to the World Hot Air Balloon Championships. The World Championships are held during odd-numbered years under the auspices of the FAI and include entrants from more than twenty nations.

Most of the activities of the BFA are concerned with keeping ballooning a safe and unfettered sport. A primary goal of the BFA is to preserve the freedom of the air for current and future pilots. This is accomplished in part by encouraging a good safety record. In keeping with this goal to promote safe ballooning, the BFA continues to propose legis-

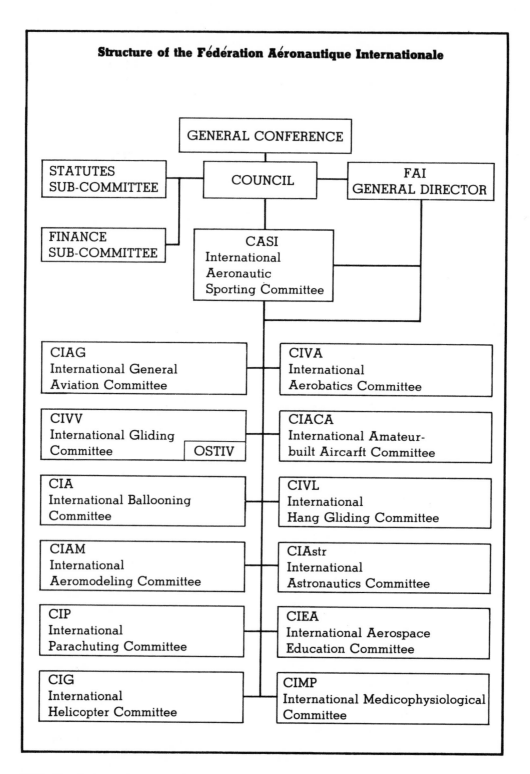

Structure of the Fédération Aéronautique Internationale

GENERAL CONFERENCE

STATUTES SUB-COMMITTEE

COUNCIL

FAI GENERAL DIRECTOR

FINANCE SUB-COMMITTEE

CASI
International Aeronautic Sporting Committee

CIAG
International General Aviation Committee

CIVA
International Aerobatics Committee

CIVV
International Gliding Committee — OSTIV

CIACA
International Amateur-built Aircarft Committee

CIA
International Ballooning Committee

CIVL
International Hang Gliding Committee

CIAM
International Aeromodeling Committee

CIAstr
International Astronautics Committee

CIP
International Parachuting Committee

CIEA
International Aerospace Education Committee

CIG
International Helicopter Committee

CIMP
International Medicophysiological Committee

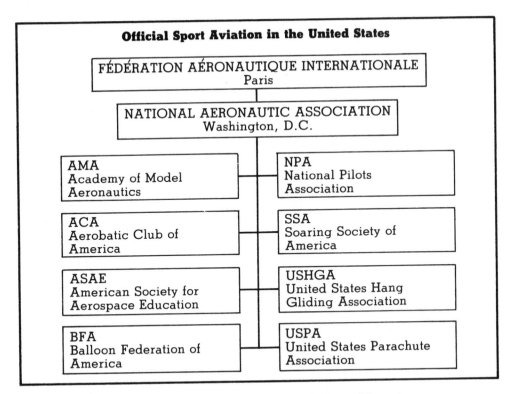

Official Sport Aviation in the United States

FÉDÉRATION AÉRONAUTIQUE INTERNATIONALE
Paris

NATIONAL AERONAUTIC ASSOCIATION
Washington, D.C.

AMA Academy of Model Aeronautics	**NPA** National Pilots Association
ACA Aerobatic Club of America	**SSA** Soaring Society of America
ASAE American Society for Aerospace Education	**USHGA** United States Hang Gliding Association
BFA Balloon Federation of America	**USPA** United States Parachute Association

lation to the Federal Aviation Administration (FAA). The BFA assists in balloon events, publishes safety guidelines, and conducts safety seminars to improve the safety of balloons and pilots. Time and effort is spent educating pilots, manufacturers, the FAA, and the public, and assisting the orderly growth of the sport.

Some BFA members have been instrumental in formulating balloon insurance policies that include unique provisions to meet the specific needs of American balloonists.

Persons interested in the sport of ballooning may join the BFA as nonpilot members, pilot members, or life members. All classes of membership include an annual subscription to *Ballooning* and all new members receive the booklet *Welcome to the Balloon Federation of America*. Voting privileges are reserved for licensed balloon pilots only. Pilot members also receive the monthly *Pilot Newsletter* and are eligible for listing in the annual pilot directory.

U.S. Balloon Manufacturers Association
c/o Raven Industries
Box 1007
Sioux Falls, S.D. 57117

This fledgling group, formed in 1979, hopes to work together in areas of manufacturing standards, flight test standards, FAA liaison, and public relations, plus other general industry concerns, which may involve flight manuals, balloon part airworthiness approvals, and ballooning regulations.

International Professional Balloon Pilots Racing Association, Inc.
20 Nassau Street
Princeton, New Jersey 08540

This group sponsored the first professional hot air balloon racing circuit in 1978. It is dedicated to the promotion of ballooning and the safety thereof.

Balloon Clubs and Associations

Alaska

Alaska Air Mushers
P.O. Box 1295
Anchorage, Alaska 99510

Arizona

Gila River and Salt River Base and Meridian
Hot Air Balloon and Airship Ascension Social
Society, Inc.
505 West Camelback Road
Phoenix, Arizona, 85013

Heads in the Clouds, Ballooning Arts
210 West Benton Avenue
Flagstaff, Arizona 86001

Arizona Balloon Club
4341 North 24th Street
Phoenix, Arizona 85016

California

Aeronaut Society
3565 Cascade Street
Napa, California 94558

Cumulo Nimbus Escadrille, Inc.
2718 Sandpiper Drive
Costa Mesa, California 92626

Redwood Empire Sport Aviation Club
2055 Marsh Road
Santa Rosa, California 95401

Sunrise Balloon
P.O. Box 6757
Santa Rosa, California 95406

Whiskey Hill-Atherton-Menlo Oaks
Ballooning and Sporting Society
P.O. Box 2247
Menlo Park, California 94025

Wind Drifters Balloon Club
2814 Empire Avenue
Burbank, California 91504

Association of Balloon and
Airship Constructors
P.O. Box 7
Rosemead, California 91770

Colorado

Colorado Balloon Club
6484 Kendall
Arvada, Colorado 80003

Pikes Peak Ballooning Society, Inc.
P.O. Box 814
Colorado Springs, Colorado 80901

Rocky Mountain Ballooning Society
7145 West Vassar
Lakewood, Colorado 80027

Connecticut

Sky Unlimited Balloon Club of
Hartford County
300 Hillfield Road
Mount Carmel, Connecticut

Florida

Miami Balloon Club
6901 SW 71st Avenue
Miami, Florida 33156

Cloud Climbers Balloon Club
2265 Middleton Avenue
Winter Park, Florida 32792

Tradewinds Balloon Club
1407 East Las Olas Boulevard
Fort Lauderdale, Florida 33301

Georgia

Georgia Balloon Association
1966 Tulane Court
Riverdale, Georgia 30274

Illinois

Chicagoland Balloon Club
Suite 400, 33 West Jackson Boulevard
Chicago, Illinois 60604

Gateway Aerostatic Association
R.R. 1, Wanda Road
East Alton, Illinois 62024

Northeastern Illinois Balloon Association
R.R. 2, Box 228A
Mundelein, Illinois 60060

Indiana

Windbaggers Balloons, Inc.,
P.O. Box 542
Carmel, Indiana 46032

Southlake Ballooning Association
P.O. Box 1662
Highland, Indiana 46322

Iowa

Chickasaw Aeronauts, Inc.
Fredericksburg, Iowa 50630

Fort Dodge Aeronauts, Inc.
1508 11th Avenue North
Fort Dodge, Iowa 50501

Kansas

Wichita Balloon Club, Inc.
9734 Birch
Wichita, Kansas 67212

Topeka Balloon Club
P.O. Box 1093
Topeka, Kansas 66603

Kansas Highwinders
8413 West Murdock
Wichita, Kansas 67212

Kentucky

Balloon Society of Kentucky
P.O. Box 22245
Louisville, Kentucky 40222

Maryland

Chesapeake Balloon Association
200 2nd Avenue SE
Glen Burnie, Maryland 21061

Michigan

Highamerica Balloon Club
P.O. Box 87
Rochester, Michigan 48063

Southeastern Michigan Balloon Association
29337 Spring Hill Lane
Southfield, Michigan 48076

West Michigan Balloon Association
6146 Thornapple River Drive
Alto, Michigan 49302

Walloon Balloon Club
P.O. Box 10
Walloon Lake, Michigan 49796

Minnesota

Twin City Balloon Club
200 West Plato Boulevard
St. Paul, Minnesota 55101

Twin Cities Balloon Club
1182 Seminole
West St. Paul, Minnesota 55118

Missouri

Gateway Aerostatic Association
2339 Weldon Parkway
St. Louis, Missouri 63141

Nebraska

Nebraska Balloon Club
11303 Oakland Drive RR21
Omaha, Nebraska 68113

New Jersey

Princeton Balloon Club, Inc.
328 Park Avenue
Scotch Plains, New Jersey 07076

New Mexico

Albuquerque Aerostat Ascension Association
6905 Hensch NE
Albuquerque, New Mexico 87107

Four Corners Aerostat Association
Box 1106
Farmington, New Mexico 87401

Ohio

Buckeye Aeronaughts
356 West Indiana Avenue
Sebring, Ohio 44672

The Lighter-than-Air Society
1800 Triplett Boulevard
Akron, Ohio 44306

Maumee Valley Balloon Association
228 West Broadway
Maumee, Ohio 43537

Oregon

Oregon Lighter Than Air Society
P.O. Box 3104
Eugene, Oregon 97403

Pennsylvania

Balloon Club of America
Swarthmore, Pennsylvania

Great Adventure Balloon Club
P.O. Box 1172
Lancaster, Pennsylvania 17605

Tennessee

Nashville Montgolfier Society
Rt. 8.
Franklin, Tennessee 37064

Texas

North Texas Ballooning Association
4320 Birchman Avenue
Fort Worth, Texas, 76107

Texas Aeronauts
14410 Carolcrest
Houston, Texas 77079

Houston Balloon Pilots Association
7826 Fairview
Houston, Texas 77041

Virginia

Chesapeake Balloon Association
11010 Bristow Road
Bristow, Virginia 22013

Wisconsin

Wisconsin Balloon Group
5149 North Woodburn Street
Milwaukee, Wisconsin 53217

Balloon Manufacturers

Avian Balloon Company
South 3722 Ridgeview Drive
Spokane, Washington 99206
(509) 928-6847

Mike Adams' Balloon Loft
P.O. Box 12168
Atlanta, Georgia 30305
(404) 261-5818

The Balloon Works
Rhyne Aerodrome
RFD 2
Statesville, North Carolina 28677
(704) 873-0503

Cameron Balloons US
3600 Elizabeth Road
Ann Arbor, Michigan 48103
(313) 995-0111

Eagle Balloons, Ltd.
Balloonport
Hanover Muni Airport
Ashland, Virginia 23005
(804) 798-8830

Don Piccard Balloons, Inc.
P.O. Box 1902
Newport Beach, California 92663
(714) 642-3545

Raven Industries, Inc.
Applied Technology Division
Box 1007
Sioux Falls, South Dakota 57117
(605) 336-2750

Skypower (gas balloons only)
Box 236
Tea, South Dakota 57064
(605) 743-2501

Thunder Balloons
75 Leonard Street
London EC2A 4QS, England

**West Coast Thunder Pacific
(Dick Pingrey)**
114 Sandalwood Court
Santa Rosa, California 95401
(707) 546-7124

**East Coast Thunder America
(Tom Gabel)**
P.O. Box 9
Lookout Mountain, Tennessee 37350
(404) 820-1641

Balloon Distributors and Dealers

ALABAMA

Balloon Works

Gary Meredith
Enterprise BalloonPort
Enterprise
(205) 347-5704

Bob Suit
Balloon World, Inc.
Birmingham
(205) 870-3988

Raven

Robert W. Woodruff II
Alabama Sport Balloons
50 Wilson Street, N.E., Suite 119
Decatur
(205) 353-7887

ALASKA

Balloon Works

Tim Brian Cooksey
Hot Air Affair
Anchorage
(907) 266-5683

Robert William Sahlman
North Star Balloons
Fairbanks
(907) 488-2652

Steven L. Tackett
Tackett Balloon Sales & Pro
Anchorage
(907) 243-5391

Raven

Mike Bauwens
Alaska Balloon Adventures
5901 Arctic Unit H
Anchorage
(907) 272-7036

ARIZONA

Balloon Works

Craig Eisenberg
Sun Devil BalloonPort
Phoenix
(602) 998-2711

Geoffrey D. Woodhouse
Hot Air West, Inc.
Phoenix
(602) 267-3268

Raven

Fred Gorrell
Cat Balloon, Inc.
2911 East Sherran Lane
Phoenix
(602) 942-2255

Ron Stewart
Aeronauts, Ltd.
5155 N. Pueblo Villas
Tucson
(602) 887-4310

Bill Miller
Arizona Balloon Co.
3003 N. Central Ave., 601
Phoenix
(602) 274-3786

ARKANSAS

Raven

Phil Wear
Balloons of Mid-America
6420 South Q Street
Fort Smith
(501) 452-5656

Bill Munday
2701 Vancouver Drive
Little Rock
(501) 227-8032

CALIFORNIA

Balloon Works

Bill Bailey
Magnificent Ascensions
Shingle Springs
(916) 677-4792

Drew Brisbane
Adventures Aloft
Yountville
(707) 255-8688

James M. Caldwell
Aerostatic Rainbow Wagons
Solana Beach
(714) 755-1301

Gary Cerveny
Dragon Balloons, Inc.
Glendale
(213) 246-5405

Michael F. Corlew
Corlew Enterprises, Balloon Div.
Fresno
(209) 435-6755

Gordon L. Hall
Hot Air Balloon Transit Co.
Covina
(213) 440-3314

Henry R. Parnell, Jr.
BalloonPort of Napa
Fairfield
(707) 425-3417

Robert Pierce
Aerostat Renaissance
Napa
(707) 226-7444

Cameron

Deke Sonnichsen
Balloons and Airships West
P.O. Box 2247
Menlo Park
(415) 323-2757

Dennis Knick
2741 Palora Avenue
Atwater
(209) 357-0823

Piccard

Dean A. Ekdahl
DAE Flights
P.O. Box 1086
Newport Beach
(714) 675-3902

Dan Glick
Sunrise Balloons
P.O. Box 571
Palm Desert
(714) 346-7591

Raven

Fred Krieg
Scorpion Productions
P.O. Box 1147
Perris
(714) 657-6930

John Wallis
S & J Balloons
54 Utah Avenue
Woodland
(916) 666-6424

John Lancaster
Air Add
27895 Washington
Winchester
(213) 796-4985

Bill Almarez
Balloons Unlimited
P.O. Box 1506
9265 Hillside Drive
Spring Valley
(714) 464-5227

Roger Barker
14728 Magnolia 2
Sherman Oaks
(213) 981-8360

Balloon Distributers and Dealers 195

Frank Jones
Dream Weaver Balloons
1781 East Woodbury Road
Pasadena
(213) 794-5470

Don Hamman
Great Western Balloons
1893 South Newcomb
Porterville
(209) 784-1790

George Haas
A Hot Air Line
5002 Olympic Drive
Los Alamitos
(213) 594-8507

Rod Duff
MacDuff's Flying Circus
45527 Saigon Avenue
Lancaster
(805) 942-5406

Jay Sutherland
Pacific Balloons of Fullerton
3814 Lariat Place
Fullerton
(714) 870-4320

Doug Treuting
Balloonacy
2610 Voorhees 4
Redondo Beach
(213) 371-8693

Bruce Keown
Piuma Aircraft Corporation
P.O. Box 1112
24800 Piuma Road
Malibu
(213) 888-0576

Brent Stockwell
Balloon Excelsior, Inc.
1241 High Street
Oakland
(415) 261-4222

Warren Haile
Sky Skimmers Balloon Company
1719 So. George Washington Blvd.
Yuba City
(916) 673-6616

Randy Kern
Marin French Balloon Co.
189 Deer Hollow
San Anselmo
(415) 454-4806

Stuart Wakeman
Sky Designs
1809 Larkin Drive
Roseville
(916) 783-4980

Thunder

Dick Pingrey
114 Sandalwood Court
Santa Rosa
(707) 546-7124

COLORADO

Balloon Works

Mike Bundgaard
Life Cycle Balloon School
Denver
(303) 759-3907

Robb R. Casseday
New Horizon Balloons
Greeley
(303) 284-5130

Alfred O. Herr
Fred Herr Sport Aviation
Fort Collins
(303) 226-0671

David Levin
Balloon Ranch
Del Norte
(303) 754-2533

Nick Saum
Raghag Balloons
Golden
(303) 278-1275

James D. Spitzer
The Balloon Barnes
Pueblo
(303) 544-6190

Leonard V. Wheatley
Great Pikes Peak Balloon Co.
Manitou Springs
(303) 473-2300 ext. 692

Cameron

Bob Kenny
1801 Lashley
Longmont
(303) 776-2860

Piccard

Raymond J. Leopold
Rocky Mountain Sport Balloons, Inc.
7350 Pure Creek Road
Colorado Springs
(303) 598-9664

Raven

Chauncey Dunn
American Balloon Adventures, Ltd.
7145 W. Vassar
Lakewood
(303) 988-7711

Tom Nevison
Magic Balloons
P.O. Box 997
Vail
(303) 476-5101

James J. Garcia
Circle Crest Enterprises
4028 Cherry Hills Dr.
Fort Collins
(303) 493-4180

Pete Peterson
Aerostation Enterprises
525 Big Sky Court
Colorado Springs
(303) 598-7078

Fred Bell
10354 Georgia Circle
Morrison
(303) 697-6250

CONNECTICUT
Cameron

Brian Boland
Pine Drive, RFD 2
Burlington
(203) 673-1307

Raven

Bill Costen
Sky Endeavors
105 Sherbrooke Avenue
Hartford
(203) 677-7811

Ray S. Cole
Olympia Balloons
18 Chimney Point
New Milford
(203) 354-1802

DELAWARE
Balloon Works

Floyd S. Cornelison, Jr.
Airborne, Inc.
Wilmington
(302) 654-8351

DISTRICT OF COLUMBIA
Cameron

Kevin Poeppelman
Atlantic Coast Balloon Company
Box 57201
Washington
(703) 660-6066

Balloon Distributers and Dealers 197

FLORIDA

Balloon Works

Alvin Dale Akridge
AA Enterprises
Fort Lauderdale
(305) 462-3852

Joe Hartley
Hot Air Promotions
South Daytona
(904) 761-2765

John B. Hickey
John Hickey & Company
Tampa
(813) 228-7645

Rick Neubauer
Balloons over Miami Co.
Miami
(304) 248-4911

Steve Roberts
Balloons Are Fun
Avon Park
(813) 453-3852

Alan E. Simonsen
Balloons over Orlando
Windermere
(305) 656-1586

Bob Snow
Phineas Phoggs Balloon Works
Orlando
(305) 422-2434

Raven

Kingswood Sprott
King Sprott Balloons
402 S. Kentucky Ave., Suite 590
Lakeland
(813) 688-6694

Colvin Rouse
Sport Balloons, Inc.
1540 North Franklin St.
Tampa
(813) 223-5787

Chuck Rohr
Rohr Balloons
110 S.W. 3rd Ave.
Fort Lauderdale
(305) 462-3852

Lee Watson
Balloons Aloft
P.O. Box 2181
Orlando
(305) 423-2181

Bill Nixon
Cirrus Air
600 Nokomis Ave. S.
Venice
(813) 485-7111

GEORGIA

Balloon Works

David Bailey
BalloonPort of Atlanta
Atlanta
(404) 996-4123

Thomas Michael Holloway
Great American Balloon Corp.
Atlanta
(404) 874-5904

Barclay Terhune
BalloonPort of Rome
Rome
(404) 235-2200

Robert Watkins
BalloonPort of North Georgia
Helen
(404) 878-2470

Raven

H. Harold Carter
Balloons, Inc.
1978 E. Roxboro Road N.E.
Atlanta
(404) 452-0010

Jerry Rainwater
Southeastern Balloon Services
Administration Bldg., Suite 221
DeKalb-Peachtree Airport
Atlanta
(404) 452-1350

IDAHO

Balloon Works

Scott Spencer
Idaho Balloon Adventures
Boise
(208) 344-5591

Raven

Fred C. Reed
Red Baron Flying Service of Driggs, Inc.
Teton Peaks Airport
Driggs
(208) 354-8131

ILLINOIS

Balloon Works

James A. Bicket
Windy City BP
Bloomington
(309) 662-3546

Alan Blount
Alan Blount Aeronaut
Palos Park
(312) 448-6100

Raymond J. Johnson
Balloons and Things, Inc.
Libertyville
(312) 793-2436

Charles King
Auburn
(217) 438-6996

Terry Stahly
BalloonPort of Illinois
Bloomington
(309) 662-1331

Dean Stellas
Windy City BalloonPort, Ltd.
Glenview
(312) 348-5721

Bob Strand
Hickory Glen BalloonPort
Mundelein
(312) 526-7524

Cameron

Ted Peterson
319 North Vine Street
Hinsdale
(312) 325-1257

Piccard

Ray Anderson
A-One Balloon Service
706 E. Washington Street
Urbana
(217) 328-2955

Douglas Blount
Great American Balloon Co.
12518 So. 82nd Avenue
Palos Park
(312) 448-3247

Raven

Russ Hardy
Illinois Balloon School
427 Ridge St.
Algonquin
(312) 658-8661

Doug Kent
Land of Lincoln Hot Air Balloon Corp.
P.O. Box 1061
Springfield
(217) 629-9613

Dick Lindquist
Forest City Balloon Co.
4214 Yale Drive
Rockford
(815) 397-4901

Allen Brown
Whittaker Balloon Company
1306 Silver 6
Urbana
(217) 384-6888

INDIANA

Balloon Works

Laurie A. Jones
Syracuse
(219) 457-2437

Peter Krieg
Peter Krieg Aeronaut
Indianapolis
(317) 255-5416

Judy Kuenning
Cloud 9 Ltd.
West Terre Haute
(812) 535-3316

Donald Menchhofer
BalloonPort of Indiana
Noblesville
(317) 849-7755

John T. Sankowski
Balloon Masters, Ltd.
Highland
(219) 844-8320

Mark Kevin Walchak
Evansville Hot Air Balloon Co.
Evansville
(812) 426-6575

Cameron

Dave Bobel
259 North Dukes
Peru
(317) 473-4534

Raven

George Green
Balloonists of Oz
Rt. 1, P.O. Box 233
Remington
(219) 261-2908

James D. Hanson
Indiana Balloons, Inc.
P.O. Box 356
Zionsville
(317) 871-4279

Ted Shafer
Balloon Enterprises
5414 S. York
South Bend
(219) 234-1063

IOWA

Balloon Works

Rob Bartholomew
Balloons over Iowa
Carlisle
(515) 989-0258

John J. Johnson
Hot Air Balloon Unlimited
Mason City
(515) 423-0675

Thomas R. Oerman
American Balloon Services, Inc.
Muscatine
(319) 264-1878

Cameron

Pete Stamats
Buzzards Glory Balloon Co.
R.R. 3, Rosedale Road S.E.
Cedar Rapids
(319) 363-3842

Piccard

Denny Cox
Special Forces Ltd.
504 Washington
Pleasantville
(515) 848-3285

Raven

Gary Ruble
Billboards in the Wind
1201 North C
Indianola
(515) 961-7045

Dave Friedley
23 South Federal
Mason City
(515) 423-5681

Dave Beukelman
1508 11th Ave. North
Fort Dodge
(515) 573-8265

Dale Points
1906 Fair Ave.
Bettendorf
(319) 797-8450

Doug Adams
Box 1434
Sioux City
(605) 232-4311

KANSAS
Balloon Works

Jerry E. Brown
Johnson County BalloonPort
Overland Park
(913) 381-1758

Gary Calvert
PB Balloon Enterprises
Wichita
(316) 263-3931

Diana G. Forshee
Pegasus Balloon Company
Wichita
(316) 265-8378

Frank Hoover
BalloonPort of Wichita
Wichita
(316) 267-2001

Kathy Hunter
Tri-Lakes BalloonPort
Wichita
(316) 265-8378

Alan Paul Miller
Lawrence BalloonPort
Lawrence
(913) 841-7700 ext 106

Sandie Spurrier
BalloonPort of Wichita
Wichita
(316) 685-8503

C. R. Tantillo
Sail-A-Way
Topeka
(913) 478-4999

Piccard

Herbert Wilcox
Balloons Aloft
209 E. Main Street
Anthony
(316) 842-3261

Raven

George Dingey
Aire Affaire, Ltd.
P.O. Box 214
Bonner Springs
(913) 422-1029

Joe Hosey
3403 Westview
Topeka
(913) 267-2705

George Hobbs
Jorg Enterprises
9356 W. Central
Wichita
(316) 722-0611

KENTUCKY
Balloon Works

Dr. Norman Cohen
Shrine Balloon Patrol
Louisville
(502) 452-9521

James Napier III
Balloon Adventures, Ltd
Bowling Green
(502) 781-6000

Richard Rys
Eye of Hurricane Ballooning Ltd.
Lexington
(606) 252-3765

Raven

Chuck Ehrler
Balloon Odyssey, Inc.
P.O. Box 33065
Louisville
(501) 245-1588

LOUISIANA

Balloon Works

Ronald L. Mills
Bayou Balloons
New Orleans
(504) 392-0032

Kirk Onderdonk
Adventures Aloft
Scott
(318) 873-6376

Raven

Don Grimes
Luziann Balloons
P.O. Box 1311
Hammond
(504) 542-1239

MAINE

Balloon Works

Virginia Geyer
Balloon Drifters, Inc.
Augusta
(207) 622-1211

Derald Young
Damn Yankee Balloon, Inc.
Newport
(207) 368-5051

Raven

Ed Cardinali
Natural High Camping and Balloon Area
Route 202
South Lebanon
(207) 339-9630

MARYLAND

Balloon Works

Gladen R. Hamilton
Annapolis BalloonPort
Edgewater
(301) 956-5436

Raven

Henry (Reds) Horrocks
Hot Air Balloon Racing Team
4100 Stansbury Mill Road
Monkton
(301) 666-1398

Jeffrey Horrocks
Nevermore Balloon Sales of Gaithersburg
Route 2, Box 65–8C
Ijamsville
(301) 831-6315

Pat Michaels
Sky High Adventures
17513 Sopher Street
Poolesville
(301) 972-7004

MASSACHUSETTS

Balloon Works

Terrance N. Mulryan
Amherst Hot Air Balloon Co.
Amherst
(413) 253-3834

Raven

Ralph Hall
Hall's Hot Air Balloon School of
Higher Learning
1656 Massachusetts Avenue
Lexington
(617) 861-0101

Dr. Clayton Thomas
Balloon School of Massachusetts
R.F.D. 1, Dingley Dell
Palmer
(413) 283-3431

Bob Kane
Blue Sky Promotions, Inc.
49 Union Street
Worcester
(617) 755-2552

MICHIGAN

Balloon Works

Gordon K. Boring
Wicker Basket Balloon Center
Livonia
(313) 425-5020

Miles Chase
Chase Farms Balloons
Walkerville
(616) 873-3337

Joseph A. DeRosa
The Hot Air Affair
Pontiac
(313) 673-3683

Dennis Kollin
Sky Adventures
Rochester
(313) 652-2067

Douglas Mills
Sky High Hot Air Balloons
Caledonia
(616) 891-8520

James J. Thornton
Titanic BalloonPort
Grand Blanc
(313) 695-0311

Cameron

Bruce & Tucker Comstock
Jeff VanAlstine
3600 Elizabeth Road
Ann Arbor
(313) 995-0111

Ted and Guy Gauthier
The Balloon Depot
1926 Woodland
Pontiac
(313) 682-3039

Bill Kaltz
9280 Dexter Town Hall Road
Pinckney
(313) 426-8024

Phil Glebe
14126 Jackson
Taylor
(313) 483-7700

Piccard

Linden Harding
Highamerica
P.O. Box 6596
2285 Starr Court
Auburn Heights
(313) 852-0666

Larry Lodenstein
2626 60th Street S.E.
Kentwood

Raven

Dennis Floden
Balloon Corporation of America
P.O. Box 3039
Flint
(313) 767-2120

Blair Mohr
Hillsdale Aero, Inc.
Box 238
Hillsdale
(517) 437-4755

Tom Bergeon
Aloft, Inc.
492 S. Edgar
Mason
(517) 327-3500

Mike Schnepp
Carson City Balloons, Inc.
P.O. Box 186
Carson City
(517) 584-3537

John C. Hall
Ballooney Tunes
1259 Ironwood
Williamston
(517) 374-3818

Wayne Warren
Bubbles, Ltd.
866 Williamsburg, Apt. 168
Pontiac
(313) 858-0987

Randy or Ron Byrne
The Peak
3150 Carpenter Road
Ypsilanti
(313) 971-4310

Dave or Paul Sgriccia
Sky Fantasy Balloons
1825 LeRene
Walled Lake
(313) 353-0830 ext 263

William Cowles
International Balloon Corp.
3561 S. Washington Ave.
Saginaw
(517) 752—6121

MINNESOTA

Balloon Works

Edward J. Chapman
Balloon Ascensions Unlimited
Prior Lake
(612) 447-5677

Cameron

Bruce Burnevik
10123 Mississippi Blvd.
Coon Rapids
(612) 755-7445

Raven

Matt Wiederkehr
Wiederkehr Balloons International, Inc.
1604 Euclid St.
St. Paul
(612) BAL-LOON

George or Greg Paul
Viking Balloon Sales
P.O. Box 248
Detroit Lakes
(218) 847-7649

George Ibach
Rochester Sport Balloons
18–7th Street N.E.
Rochester
(507) 285-0283

Brian Burnevik
Ad-Air Balloons
10844 Butternut St.
Coon Rapids
(612) 755-0683

Earl Richards
Fantasy Flights
1602 Maple Grove Rd.
Duluth
(218) 727-2784

MISSISSIPPI

Balloon Works

Jerry Bagley
Airad Inc.
Jackson
(601) 944-0467

Raven

Herbert Smith
Mississippi Ascensions
112 Swallow Drive
Brandon
(601) 355-3147

John Weathersby
Weathersby Enterprises
P.O. Box 880
Indianola
(601) 887-2711

MISSOURI

Balloon Works

Nikki Caplan
BalloonPort of St. Louis
St. Louis
(314) 878-3211

Allan L. Coon
Ozark Mountain BP
Branson
(913) 782-1190

Ronald D. Regan
Balloon Fantasies Ltd.
Kansas City
(816) 753-1367

Dr. Gary Sines
BalloonPort of Kansas City
Holt
(816) 896-5127

Raven

Ted Staley
Mississippi River Transit Co.
130 E. Jefferson
St. Louis
(314) 822-1122

Dave Livengood
2317 East Grandview
Springfield
(417) 833-4651

MONTANA

Balloon Works

Ralph Giantz, Jr.
Billings
(406) 259-7919

Piccard

Tom Barrow
Rocky Mountain BalloonPort
P.O. Box 21079
Billings
(406) 259-1038

Raven

Dr. John Richardson
J.W.R. Enterprises
12 Hidden Valley Rd.
Havre
(406) 265-5922

NEBRASKA

Balloon Works

John D. Folsom
Aeronautical Adventures
Grand Island
(308) 382-7970

Donald J. Hays
Horizon Balloon Company
Omaha
(402) 399-2200

David Hollenbaugh
Grasshopper Balloon Company
Lincoln
(402) 470-3333

Piccard

Rich White
13229 Glen Street
Papillion
(402) 895-2536

Raven

Donna Gloshen
Gloshen Balloons, Inc.
4725 South 184th Plaza
Omaha
(402) 330-2770

NEVADA

Raven

Bill Busse
Balloon Hanger
2445 Apricot Lane
Las Vegas
(702) 647-3202

NEW JERSEY
Balloon Works
Dennis Fleck
Garden State BalloonPort
Far Hills
(201) 234-0547

James Mount
Looking Up Advertising, Inc.
North Plainfield
(201) 889-5084

Raven
Robert L. Waligunda
Balloon Enterprises, Inc.
20 Nassau Street
Princeton
(609) 921-6636

NEW MEXICO
Balloon Works
Ron Clifford
Timothy Darrin
Adventures Aloft
Albuquerque
(505) 881-2310

John Davis, IV
BalloonPort of Albuquerque
Albuquerque
(505) 292-2958

Michael L. English
San Juan Aerostats
Farmington
(505) 327-5097

Darryl Gunter
Aerco
Albuquerque
(505) 344-5423

Warren A. Hill
BalloonPort of Santa Fe
Santa Fe
(505) 983-7384

Robert John
Albuquerque
(505) 268-2886

Ms. Paula O'Brien
Barnestomers
Albuquerque
(505) 247-9501 ext 300

Raven
Sid Cutter
World Balloon Corporation
4800 Eubank, N.E.
Albuquerque
(505) 293-6800

Ron Slonaker
Four Corners Balloons
P.O. Box 2406
Farmington
(505) 327-4575

Doug March
Southwestern Balloon Adventures
6905 Hensch, N.E.
Albuquerque
(505) 298-1891

Alan Wilson
Mesa Balloon Ascensions
923 Ute Circle
Gallup
(505) 722-4259

Bill Flynt
111 E. 22nd, Apt. 101
Roswell
(505) 622-1275

NEW YORK
Balloon Works
Robert Auchincloss
Great Hot Air Balloon Emporium
Poughkeepsie
(914) 454-5132

James C. Benson
BalloonPort of Rochester
Rochester
(716) 254-5050

James Griswold
Fantasy Flights
Manlius
(315) 682-2575

George T. Lewis
Great Hot Air Balloon Emporium
Hughsonville
(914) 686-3057

Dana R. Pickup
Great Hot Air Balloon Emporium
Olean
(716) 372-3206

David S. Steven
Star Balloons
Chatham
(518) 392-3208

Cameron

Michael McGee
90 Potter Avenue
Orchard Park
(716) 846-8387

Raven

David L. Weston Associates
7601 Daphne Drive
North Syracuse
(315) 452-0482

Roy Webb
Nature Balloons
P.O. Box 334
Watkins Glen
(607) 535-9526

Clotaire F. Castanier
Skyworks
211 W. 56th Avenue Apt. 16E
New York
(212) 765-0957

Phil Jackson
Adirondack Balloon Transit Ltd.
Box 65
Glens Falls
(518) 793-6342

Walt Griskot
Adirondack Hot Air Balloon Festival, Inc.
P.O. Box 883
Glens Falls
(518) 792-2600

Mark Laurin
Airborne Adventures
317 Chestnut Street
North Syracuse
(315) 458-3305

Harris Gordon
Up, Up, and Away
P.O. Box 32
Monticello
(914) 583-7030

Sam Cali
Greenbush Aviation
189 Valley Road
Katonah
(914) 694-8383

Tony Von Elbe
Clinton Aero Corporation
Box 367
Plattsburg
(518) 561-4350

Dave Peebles
Global Ascension Signs
30 Upper Loudon Road
Loudonville
(518) 465-9449

Carroll Teitsworth
Liberty Balloon Corporation
6699 Barber Hill Road
Groveland
(716) 243-3178

NORTH CAROLINA

Balloon Works

James Cunningham Buie
By Mutual Ascent, Inc.
Raleigh
(919) 781-4873

Jo Ann Cline
Carolina Cloudchasers BP
Greensboro
(919) 852-2450

Johnson Davis
Professional Balloonist
Winston-Salem
(919) 723-7296

Harold K. Jolly
Balloons Everywhere Ltd.
Durham
(919) 477-2141

William E. Norwood
Land "O" Sky Aeronautics
Skyland
(704) 255-0013

Mike Shouse
Balloon Ascensions
Statesville
(704) 876-1236

OHIO

Balloon Works

Kenneth Austin
Austin Aircraft
Medina
(216) 239-2678

Lucinda Gates
Second Wind Aerostation
Garrettsville
(216) 548-4511

Gerald W. Geisen
Balloons Unlimited, Inc.
Cincinnati
(513) 474-2808

Arch Hawkins
FF BalloonPort of Sebring
Sebring
(216) 823-3295

Edward R. Lappies
Ballooning Adventures
Grand River
(216) 357-0035

Stephen Laudick
Van Wert BalloonPort
Van Wert
(419) 238-9741

Gary Meddock
BalloonPort of Dayton
Dayton
(513) 434-0530

Gene H. Tabbert
The Balloon Company
Maumee
(419) 866-1841

Cameron

Al Nels
1588 Edenwood Drive
Xenia
(513) 426-6014

Bud Newhouse
415 S. Liberty-Keuter
Lebanon
(513) 721-1660

Raven

Steve & Denny Shiels
Skysigns Unlimited
1734 Dexter Ave.
Cincinnati
(513) 871-4564

Bill Lauro
Sky Sailors Balloon Port
733 Beechview Dr.
Akron
(216) 784-1307

Eric E. Barnum
Falcon Aeronautical, Inc.
Toldeo-Metcalf Airport 28331
LeMoyne
(419) 838-6921

Gary Klein
Western Reserve Flying Machine Co.
61 E. Streetsboro
Hudson
(216) 653-6471

Jim Birk
Tri-State Balloons
1300 Powell View Drive
Defiance
(419) 784-4010

OKLAHOMA

Balloon Works

Jimmy M. Mitchell
Aerodyne, Inc.
Tulsa
(918) 749-3171

Gregory Thompson
Sooner Balloon Corp.
Moore
(405) 794-7277

Raven

Ron Thompson
Balloon Ascensions, Inc.
1027 W. K Street
Jenks
(918) 299-5535

Darrell Duer
Duer, Inc.
5826 N.E. 63rd
Oklahoma City
(405) 721-2525

OREGON
Balloon Works

John R. Canfield
The Balloon, Inc.
Eugene
(503) 485-4191

Christopher P. Kirby
Oregon Balloon Ventures, Inc.
Tigard
(503) 643-7661

Cameron

Deke Sonnichsen
Balloons & Airships West
P.O. Box 3853
Eugene
(415) 323-2757

Raven

Roger Kleve
Aries Enterprises, Ltd.
3660 Mariposa
Albany
(503) 926-6462

Jim Ricci
Sun Country Aviation
63445 Deschutes Mkt. Rd.
Bend
(503) 382-1902

Greg Guy
Balloon Ascensions of Oregon
1865 19th Street N.E.
Salem
(503) 362-2874

Jim Pope
Blue Sky Balloons
1680 Brookhurst St.
Medford
(503) 779-9543

John Cox
Northwest Aviation Enterprises
P.O. Box 468
Portland
(503) 228-0089

PENNSYLVANIA

Balloon Works

Dale Fleck
Garden State BalloonPort
State College
(814) 234-6451

Cameron

Jerry Spaulding
1425 Ponds Edge Road
West Chester
(215) 696-5433

Piccard

Lawrence Gehrlein
Thermal G. Gliderport
9001 Hamot Road, RD 4
Waterford
(814) 866-1131

John R. Hager
357 Old Delp Road
Lancaster
(717) 569-1700

Raven

John Addison
The Pit Stop
149 Arch Street
Greensburg
(413) 836-5530

Richard Blum
Aerostatic Enterprises
1211 Highland Avenue
Fort Washington
(215) 368-1533

RHODE ISLAND

Balloon Works

Steve Audette
Blue Ridge BalloonPort
Newport
(401) 849-2518

SOUTH DAKOTA

Balloon Works

Ned E. Wick
Wick Promotions Limited
Rapid City
(605) 342-8262

Ed Yost
Universal Systems Corp.
Tea
(605) 743-2501

Raven

Orvin Olivier
North Central Aero Sports
709 S. Bahnson
Sioux Falls
(605) 332-6688

Dave McPherson
Black Hills Airesport
P.O. Box 126
Sturgis
(605) 347-3811

TENNESSEE

Balloon Works

Wm. B. Anderson
Captain D's
Tullahoma
(615) 455-1692

David D. Broyles
BalloonPort of Memphis
Memphis
(901) 369-3600

David C. Eastland
Aerostation Ltd., Inc.
Franklin
(615) 373-7865

Eugene L. Johnson
Sundance Balloons
Memphis
(901) 369-3600 ext 3045

Gary F. Trew
Memphis Balloon Works
Memphis
(901) 523-2935

Cameron

Tom Lempicke
Balloon Activities, Inc.
3647 Haughton Lane 2
Memphis
(901) 388-1667

Raven

Bill Cunningham
Balloons, Planes and Things, Inc.
762 Patterson
Memphis
(901) 327-6311

Andy Anderson
North American Balloons
P.O. Box 847
Franklin
(615) 298-3338

Thunder

Tom Gabel
P.O. Box 9
Lookout Mountain
(404) 820-1641

TEXAS

Balloon Works

Dr. Bill Bussey
Longview BalloonPort
Longview
(214) 758-5551

Bill Coleman
Airship Corp. of America
Tyler
(214) 593-4488

John M. Compton
Valley Balloon Company
Mission
(512) 585-2382

William G. Davison
Pretty Balloons Unlimited
Houston
(713) 224-1060

Ray Gallager
Airship Corp. of America
West Fort Worth
(214) 593-4488

Ronny Long
BalloonPort of the SW
Grand Prairie
(214) 263-6197

Dudley R. Mann
Western Skies BalloonPort, Inc.
El Paso
(915) 544-1744

James E. Marshall
Balloon Academy of Texas
Plano
(214) 368-7009

J. C. Meador
The Meador Company
Houston
(713) 644-1206

Cameron

Terry Cooper
P.O. Box 6395
Tyler
(214) 561-7505

Piccard

John W. Collins
Great Southwest Hot Air Balloon Co., Inc.
714 Forest Trace
Rockwell
(214) 722-3601

Joseph E. Masini
Wind Wizards
4304 Donnybrook Place
El Paso
(915) 545-1649

Bill Murtorff
Rainbow's End BalloonPort
7826 Fairview
Houston
(713) 466-1927

Raven

Portis Wooley
BalloonPort of Texas
905 S. Jupiter
Garland
(214) 494-1408

Bill Hardin
Balloon Adventures
2002 Auburn Drive
Richardson
(214) 987-0303

Don Weiler
Balloon Adventures
8700 Woodway 129
Houston
(713) 780-0711

Ken Kelley
Aerostats Unlimited
Route 1, Box 400
Amarillo
(806) 353-3553

Jim Marshall
The Balloon Academy of Texas
P.O. Box 326
Plano
(214) 596-4606

Steve Jones
Cen-Tex Balloons
c/o Belco Mfg. Co.
Taylors Valley Road
Belton
(817) 939-5887

UTAH

Balloon Works

Stewart Roberts
Salt Lake BalloonPort
Salt Lake City
(801) 583-3120

VERMONT

Raven

Jack DuBrul
The Airmaster
1835 Shelbourne Road
South Burlington
(802) 864-0544

VIRGINIA

Balloon Works

Chip Dennis
The Sky Is the Limit, Inc.
Lynchburg
(804) 237-5211

William J. Jaxtheimer
Fly High Bros. Sport Balloons, Inc.
Oakton
(703) 938-2866

Michael J. Kohler
Ascension Dimension
Bristow
(703) 631-0423

Cameron

Rick Behr
813 South Pitt Street
Alexandria
(703) 683-6640

WASHINGTON

Balloon Works

Dennis Bradley
Ascensions Northwest
Bellevue
(206) 246-4722

Piccard

Nancy Ripley
Aloft Ltd.
P.O. Box 15628
Seattle
(206) 362-5040

Raven

Bill Karras
Hot Air Promotions
13919 S.E. 38th Place
Bellevue
(206) 747-9238

Bill Lloyd
Void Enterprises
1440 S. 3rd
Walla Walla
(509) 525-4110

Jon Ackerman
Cascade Pacific Balloon Company
Rink Building
3rd and Old Pacific Highway
LaCenter
(206) 263-2111

WEST VIRGINIA

Balloon Works

I.V. Cunningham, Jr.
Fox Fire Balloon Promotions, Inc.
Milton
(304) 743-5622

John Robert Hanway
Overhead Attractions
Fairmont
(304) 363-8400

Joseph M. Holt, Jr.
Greenbrier Balloon, Inc.
Lewisburg
(304) 645-6036

Jim B. Willis
West Virginia Balloon Company
Huntington
(304) 345-1999

WISCONSIN

Balloon Works

John C. Rowe
Romega Balloons
Madison
(608) 845-8777

Thomas A. Sheppard
Brit Industries, Inc.
West Bend
(414) 338-2300

Piccard

Don Janke
Hot Air Specialists
1210 Sweeny Drive
Middleton
(608) 836-7676

Raven

Dick Gnant
Up and Away
2385 N. Calhoun Road
Brookfield
(414) 782-6758

Dan Beecroft
Majestic Flight
Route 2, Box 109
Frederic
(715) 653-2635

Mike Carlile
5501 Winnequah Rd.
Madison
(608) 222-6318

Jeff Wingad
Horizon Adventures
Box 1082
Eau Claire
(715) 874-5040

WYOMING

Raven

Bill Grosz
2925 Garden Creek
Casper
(307) 235-1561

CANADA

Cameron

Chuck Bump
Trans-Canada Balloons Ltd.
11988 Yeo Road
R.R. 1
Ruskin, British Columbia
VOM 1RO
(604) 462-7889

Raven

Larry Horack
Cross Canada Balloons
255 Indian Road
Toronto, Ontario
M6R 2X3
(416) 649-2555

Gary Brady
Ballooning Adventures of Quebec
3676 Route 220
St. Elie d'Orford, Quebec
JOB-2S0
(819) 567-5392

John Bauman
Aerial Promotions
85 Grandin Village
St. Albert, Alberta
58N-1R9
(403) 458-5452

Mac Millar
Fly by Night Balloon Co., Ltd.
11111–105th Avenue
Edmonton, Alberta
(403) 426-1761

Kim Young
Vanguard Balloons, Ltd.
1522 McKercher Drive
Saskatoon, Saskatchewan
S7H-5E1
(306) 373-1044

Al Russell
Halton Hills BalloonPort
Blythlee Farm
R.R. 1
Acton, Ontario
L7J-2L7
(519) 853-1009

Ballooning Periodicals

Ballooning
2226 Beebee Street
San Luis Obispo, California 93401

Brian Lawler, Editor
Published every other month, this attractive, colorful magazine features stories written by members, innovations in the sport balloon industry, technological and record-making feats in the lighter-than-air field, and the historic events, customs, and traditions of ballooning. In addition, it provides a schedule of balloon rallies and flying festivals and commercial advertisements from manufacturers, pilot training schools, and individual traders.

The only publication of its kind in the United States, *Ballooning* is ideal for the armchair aeronaut who enjoys reading about the beauty and serenity of LTA flight, the prospective pilot seeking more information, and sport flyers and serious professionals who wish to keep abreast of the latest developments in the sport.

Aerostat
Kimberly House
Vaughan Way
Leicester, England

The equivalent of *Ballooning* in America, this is the official journal of the British Balloon and Airship Club.

Pilot Newsletter
Balloon Federation of America
Suite 430
821 Fifteenth Street N.W.
Washington, D.C. 20005

All pilot members of the BFA receive briefings on technical developments and current events in ballooning through the monthly *Pilot Newsletter*. The newsletter also covers competitive flying, changes in federal regulations pertaining to balloon flying, a classified-ad exchange column, Federation minutes and business, and other items of interest to those within the ballooning community.

Buoyant Flight
The Lighter-Than-Air Society
1800 Triplett Boulevard
Akron, Ohio 44306

This newsletter covers blimp and balloon activity, with a heavy accent on airship history.

Raven Owners Newsletter
P.O. Box 1007
Sioux Falls, South Dakota 57117

Monthly newsletter devoted to matters of general interest as well as to some technical subjects relating especially to Raven balloons.

Balloon Museums

National Air and Space Museum
Smithsonian Institution
Independence Avenue between
4th and 7th Streets, S.W.
Washington, D.C. 20560

The largest objects in the Balloon/Airship Hall, one of a dozen major permanent exhibitions in this dazzling new museum, are the eight-foot spherical cabin used in the 1936 record-breaking stratospheric ascent co-sponsored by the office of Naval Research and the National Geographic Society, the *Hindenburg* car reproduction, the *Pilgrim* car, and a Curtis Sparrowhawk aeroplane actually used on the *Akron* airship. At either end of the hall's south side are two twenty by twenty-foot main floor-to-roof bays, each displaying a balloon. One, built by Bob Sparks, is a two-fifths scale model of the first manned montgolfier. A silent fan keeps the montgolfier inflated. In the other bay hangs the *America*, a quarter-scale modern hot air balloon, built and donated by Bob Waligunda.

Back in the hall itself, the visitor will see, among other things, a small charlière, the first manned gas balloon, and another small copy of the first montgolfier, rising up and down above a heated duct. Both six to eight-foot diameter models were also built by Sparks.

The newest and most exciting display is the gondola of the *Double Eagle II*, the first balloon to cross the Atlantic.

Other display items include the following: a pictorial display of rare original prints of the Balloomania period; a collection of chinaware, medallions, etc., of the same period; a furnished balloon room with priceless eighteenth and early nineteenth century furniture in it; a collection of prints of early dirigibles (mostly impractical ideas); a wicker basket; an animated theater of the first channel crossing by Blanchard and Jeffries; a Santos-Dumont display; a Buoyant Flight in War display; high altitude ballooning and sport ballooning exhibits; balloon comparison pictures and art; a NOAA radiosonde balloon exhibit; a wide variety of rigid airship models, pictures, memorabilia, posters, mail, baggage tags, girders, fabric, etc; a *Hindenburg* Room with some surviving Universal Studios film furniture, table settings, etc.; the large model of the *Hindenburg* suspended from the ceiling; a U.S. Navy blimp panel with charts and pictures; modern blimp operations shown by models; a panel showing various Atlantic crossing attempts; another panel showing futuristic airship notions; and, at the exit area, a modern hot air balloon basket and a large back-illuminated multipanel display of hot air balloons.

Musée des Ballons
Château de Balleroy
Normandy, France
c/o *Forbes* Magazine
60 Fifth Avenue
New York, N.Y. 10011

The first museum in the world devoted entirely to the science, art, and sport of ballooning was officially opened in Balleroy, France, on May 31, 1975. The museum, sponsored by *Forbes* Magazine, is situated on the grounds of Normandy's magnificent Château de Balleroy, a few miles southwest of Bayeux.

The museum currently occupies one of two buildings on either side of the floral gardens at the Château. The gardens are at the end of a long drive which leads directly to the main road of the village of Balleroy. The Château grounds, designated by the French government as an official balloon port, are surrounded by Norman farmland and deciduous forests. Designed by Francois Mansart and built in 1626, the Château features precision stonework and an interior decorated with numerous paintings by Count Albert de Balleroy.

It is expected that the Balloon Museum

will attract many visitors since it is so closely situated near the D-Day beaches.

Attempted Atlantic crossings are featured in the Musee des Ballons where the *Windborne* gondola, equipment, and rigging, and many photos of the aborted launch are on display. There is also a display of scientific balloons, consisting of photos and equipment contributed by the Centre National d'Études Spatiales (CNES).

Most exhibits are historical in nature. There is a *nacelle* or gondola, from a five- to six-hundred cubic-meter free balloon of 1880–1890 vintage, hanging from the ceiling. There's a large circular basket mounted on one wall. This *nacelle* is all that remains of a captive balloon used at a French commercial exposition in 1904.

On another wall there are several prints of early 1900 French ballooning and the record flight of Vincennes Korostichew of Russia who, in 1900, flew 1,925 kilometers in thirty-five hours, forty-five minutes. There are wall prints of aeronauts Count de la Vaulx and Alberto Santos-Dumont, and other unique paintings and plaques. And there is a fledging new library on aerostation.

There are three dioramas: one depicts the 1870 Siege of Paris; one shows the first flight of the balloon *Chateau de Balleroy* on September 25, 1973, in France; and one illustrates the November 21, 1783, flight by Pilâtre de Rosier and Marquis d'Arlandes at the Château de la Muette, titled *Le Premier Envol* ("The First Takeoff").

Upstairs, in the loft, there are numerous photos, medals, and other balloon memorabilia, featuring such famous early aeronauts as Étienne de Montgolfier (1745–1799), Joseph de Montgolfier (1740–1811), and Jacques Alexandre César Charles (1746–1823). There are artifacts and prints of various flights starting with the 1780's: Madame Blanchard, Le Geant and Nadar, the Royal Nassau balloon, Professor Wise (1808–1879), Prof. T. S. C. Lowe, Professor Piccard, and a load ring from the Siege of Paris.

There are other items, too: a collection of porcelain plates depicting the history of ballooning from 1783 to 1814; some pieces of a German zeppelin that crashed in England on September 3, 1916; more *nacelles*, including one from the Renard-type 980 cubic-meter military balloons; and other window displays of Capt. Jean Coutelle, who at the battle of Fleurus in 1794 made the first military balloon ascension. Also, there are some memorabilia on A. Holland Forbes, the first president of the Aero Club of America, and his balloon *New York*. Forbes and Auguste Post narrowly escaped death in Berlin on December 13, 1910, when their balloon deflated at an altitude of 1,000 meters.

On the more modern side of ballooning history, there is a beautiful display of barrage balloons and some photographs of the first flight across the English Channel "*en balloon a air chaud*" (in a hot air balloon) on April 13, 1963, by Ed Yost and Don Piccard. Their flight time was three hours, seventeen minutes. Also, there are mementos of Forbes' transcontinental flight and of Tracy Barnes' record flight to 37,000 feet on May 10, 1964, in a 13,800-cubic-foot polyethylene balloon.

BFA Balloon Museum
711 Northeast Street
Indianola, Iowa 50125
(515) 961-6880

This museum recently founded near the campus of Simpson College, is small but intent on growing. Present plans call for revolving exhibitions designed around such themes as the National Hot Air Balloon Championships, which are held in Indianola every year. Of special interest are its collection of photos and artifacts of the smoke-ballooning feats of Capt. Eddie Allen and "Reckless Ruby."

U.S. Air Force Museum
Wright-Patterson Air Force Base
Dayton, Ohio 45433
(513) 255-3284

There is a small but interesting permanent balloon exhibition here, which includes a scale model of the original Montgolfier balloon and numerous photos and artifacts of ballooning in the Civil War and World War I. Highlight of the exhibition (and alone worth the visit) is a fully inflated ninety-foot-high English-made Caquot balloon used by the American Balloon Corps during World War I. The museum is located six miles northeast of downtown Dayton.

U.S. Naval Aviation Museum
Naval Air Station
Pensacola, Florida 32508
(904) 452-3604

A major lighter-than-air permanent exhibition is planned. At this writing, coverage of balloons is confined to brief mention in the exhibit tracing aviation history generally.

All-Time Ballooning Records

NATIONAL HOT AIR BALLOON CHAMPIONSHIP RESULTS

Year	No. of Entrants	Site	Winners
1970	11	Des Moines, Iowa	Frank Pritchard Flint, Michigan
1971	17	Indianola, Iowa	Dennis Floden Fling, Michigan
1972	43	Indianola, Iowa	Bruce Comstock Ann Arbor, Michigan
1973	86	Indianola, Iowa	Tom Gabel Eureka, Illinois
1974	168	Indianola, Iowa	Chuck Ehrler Louisville, Kentucky
1975	199	Indianola, Iowa	Dave Medema Twin Lake, Michigan
1976	215	Indianola, Iowa	Bruce Comstock Ann Arbor, Michigan
1977	182	Indianola, Iowa	Bruce Comstock Ann Arbor, Michigan
1978	210	Indianola, Iowa	Sid Cutter Albuquerque, New Mexico
1979	318	Indianola, Iowa	Bruce Comstock Ann Arbor, Michigan
1980	340	Indianola, Iowa	Steve Jones Belton, Texas

WORLD HOT AIR BALLOON CHAMPIONSHIP

Year	No. of Entrants	Site	Winners
1973	32	Albuquerque, N.M.	1. Dennis Floden, U.S.A. 2. Bill Cutter, U.S.A. 3. Janne Balkedal, Sweden
1975	34	Albuquerque, N.M.	1. David Schaffer, U.S.A. 2. Janne Balkedal, Sweden 3. Peter Vizzard, Australia

WORLD HOT AIR BALLOON CHAMPIONSHIP

Year	No. of Entrants	Site	Winners
1977	51	York, England	1. Paul Woessner, U.S.A. 2. Bruce Comstock, U.S.A. 3. Michael Scudder, U.S.A.
1979	33	Uppsala, Sweden	1. Paul Woessner, U.S.A. 2. Sid Cutter, U.S.A. 3. Olivier Roux Devillas, France

GORDON BENNETT RACE (GAS BALLOONS)

Date	No. of Entrants	Launch Site	Destination	Duration (hours)	Distance (kilometers)	Winning Balloons
Sept. 30, 1906	16	Paris, France	Fylingdales Moor, Yorkshire, England	22	647	*United States:* Frank P. Lahm H. B. Hersey (U.S.A.)
Oct. 21, 1907	9	St. Louis, Missouri	Bradley Beach, New Jersey	40	1403	*Pommern:* Oskar Erbsloh Henry P. Clayton (Germany)
Oct. 1, 1908	23	Berlin, Germany	Bergen, Norway	73	1212	*Helvetia:* Col. Schaeck Lt. Messner (Switzerland)
Oct. 3, 1909	17	Zurich, Switzerland	Ostroleko, Poland	35	1121	*America II:* Edgar W. Mix A. Roussel (U.S.A.)
Oct. 7, 1910	10	St. Louis, Missouri	Peribonka River, Quebec, Canada	44	1884	*America II:* Alan R. Hawley August Post (U.S.A.)
Oct. 9, 1911	7	Kansas City, Missouri	Holcombe, Wisconsin	12	758	*Berlin II:* Lt. Hans Gericke O. Dunker (Germany)
Oct. 7, 1912	22	Stuttgart, Germany	Riga U.S.S.R.	46	2191	*Lapicardie:* Maurice Bienaimé R. Rumpelmayer (France)
Oct. 2, 1913	18	Paris, France	Bampton, Devonshire, England	43	618	*Goodyear:* Ralph H. Upson R.A.L. Preston (U.S.A.)
1914–1919	No Meetings		::	::	::	::

GORDON BENNETT RACE. GAS BALLOONS (continued)

Date	No. of Entrants	Launch Site	Destination	Duration (hours)	Distance (kilometers)	Winning Balloons
Oct. 3, 1920	7	Birmingham, Alabama	North Hero, Grand Island, Vermont	40	1760	*Belgica:* Ernest Demuyter M. Labrousse (Belgium)
Sept. 18, 1921	15	Brussels, Belgium	Lambay Island, Ireland	27	766	*Zurich:* Capt. Paul Armbruster Ansermier (Switzerland)
Aug. 6, 1922	19	Geneva, Switzerland	Oknitsa, Romania	25	1372	*Belgica:* Ernest Demuyter A. Veenstra (Belgium)
Sept. 23, 1923	16	Brussels, Belgium	Skollersta, Sweden	21	1115	*Belgica:* Ernest Demuyter L. Coeckelbergh (Belgium)
June 15, 1924	17	Brussels, Belgium	St. Abb's Head Scotland	43	714	*Belgica:* Ernest Demuyter L. Coeckelbergh (Belgium)
June 7, 1925	19	Brussels, Belgium	Cabo Toriñana, Spain	47	1345	*Prince Leopold:* A. Veenstra Ph. Quersin (Belgium)
May 30, 1926	17	Antwerp, Belgium	Sölvesborg, Sweden	16	861	*Goodyear III:* Ward T. Van Orman Walter W. Morton (U.S.A.)
Sept. 10, 1927	15	Detroit, Michigan	Baxley, Georgia	--	1198	*Detroit:* Edward J. Hill A. G. Schlosser (U.S.A.)
June 30, 1928	12	Detroit, Michigan	Kenbridge, Virginia	48	740	*U.S. Army:* Capt. W. E. Kepner W. O. Earickson (U.S.A.)

GORDON BENNETT RACE, GAS BALLOONS (continued)

Date	No. of Entrants	Launch Site	Destination	Duration (hours)	Distance (kilometers)	Winning Balloons
Sept. 28, 1929	9	St. Louis, Missouri	Troy, Ohio	--	548	*Goodyear VIII:* Ward T. Van Orman Alan L. MacCracken (U.S.A.)
Sept. 1, 1930	6	Cleveland, Ohio	Norfolk, Massachusetts	--	872	*Goodyear VIII:* Ward T. Van Orman Alan L. MacCracken (U.S.A.)
1931	No Meetings	--	--	--	--	--
Sept. 25, 1932	17	Basel, Switzerland	Wilno, Poland (now Vilnius, U.S.S.R.)	41	1536	*U.S. Navy:* T. G. M. Settle W. Bushnell (U.S.A.)
Sept. 2, 1933	7	Chicago, Illinois	Province of Quebec, Canada	--	1361	*Kosciusko:* Francyzek Hynek Zbigniew Burzynski (Poland)
Sept. 23, 1934	8	Warsaw, Poland	Anna Woronez, U.S.S.R.	44	1331	*Kosciusko:* Francyzek Hynek W. Pomaski (Poland)
Sept. 15, 1935	10	Warsaw, Poland	Tiszkino Stalingrad, U.S.S.R.	57	1650	*Polonia II:* Zbigniew Burzynski Wladyslaw Wysochi (Poland)
Aug. 29, 1936	10	Warsaw, Poland	Archangel'sk, U.S.S.R.	--	1715	*Belgica:* Ernest Demuyter P. Hoffmann (Belgium)
June 20, 1937	12	Brussels, Belgium	Tukumo, Lithuania	46	1396	*Belgica:* Ernest Demuyter P. Hoffmann (Belgium)

GORDON BENNETT RACE, GAS BALLOONS (continued)

Date	No. of Entrants	Launch Site	Destination	Duration (hours)	Distance (kilometers)	Winning Balloons
Sept. 11, 1938	11	Liège, Belgium	Troyan, Bulgaria	37	1692	*L.O.P.P.:* Antoni Janusz Janik (Poland)
May 26, 1979	18	Long Beach, California	Dove Creek Colorado	47	932	*Double Eagle III:* Ben Abruzzo Maxie Anderson (U.S.A.)
April 26, 1980	12	Fountain Valley, California	Leggett, California	--	528.5 (miles)	*Cloud Dancer:* Jerry Tepper Corky Meyers

All-Time Ballooning Records
for Altitude, Distance, and Duration

CLASS A — BALLOONS

Sub-Class A-1
Less than 250 Cubic Meters

7/24/60	ALTITUDE Donald L. Piccard Piccard S-10 *Holiday* balloon Minneapolis, Minnesota	U.S.A.	1,140 Meters	(3,740 Feet)
8/12/72	DISTANCE Wilma Piccard Piccard S-10 *Holiday* balloon Indianola, Iowa	U.S.A.	28.33 KMS	(17.60 Miles)

DURATION: No Official Record Established

Sub-Class A-2
Between 250 and 400 Cubic Meters

8/24/62	ALTITUDE Donald L. Piccard *Sioux City Sue* balloon Sioux City, Iowa	U.S.A.	5,409.28 Meters	(17,747 Feet)
5/3/53	DISTANCE Audouin Dollfus *Zodiac* F. AIFA balloon Senlis to Cheverny, France	France	208.622 KMS	(129.631 Miles)
5/3/53	DURATION Audouin Dollfus *Zodiac* F. AIFA balloon Senlis to Cheverny, France	France	4 Hours 00 Minutes	

Sub-Class A-3
Between 400 and 600 Cubic Meters

5/10/64	ALTITUDE Tracy Barnes Barnes 14-A balloon Rosemount, Minnesota	U.S.A.	11,780 Meters	(38,650 Feet)
7/1/22	DISTANCE Georges Cormier	France	804.173 KMS	(499.69 Miles)
3/30/41	DURATION Serge Sinoveev URSS-VR 80 balloon Dolgoprudny, USSR	U.S.S.R.	46 Hours 10 Minutes	

Sub-Class A-4
Between 600 and 900 Cubic Meters

5/10/64	ALTITUDE Tracy Barnes Barnes 14-A balloon Rosemount, Minnesota	U.S.A.	11,730 Meters	(38,650 Feet)
4/3/39	DISTANCE F. Bourlouski Moscow to Charaboulski, U.S.S.R.	U.S.S.R.	1,701.81 KMS	(1,056.95 Miles)
4/3/39	DURATION F. Bourlouski Moscow to Charaboulski, U.S.S.R.	U.S.S.R.	61 Hours 30 Minutes	

Sub-Class A-5
Between 900 and 1,200 Cubic Meters

5/10/64	ALTITUDE Tracy Barnes Barnes 14-A balloon Rosemount, Minnesota	U.S.A.	11,780 Meters	(38,650 Feet)
4/3/39	DISTANCE F. Bourlouski Moscow to Charaboulski, U.S.S.R.	U.S.S.R.	1,701.81 KMS	(1,056.95 Miles)
4/3/39	DURATION F. Bourlouski Moscow to Charaboulski, U.S.S.R.	U.S.S.R.	61 Hours 30 Minutes	

Sub-Class A-6
Between 1,200 and 1,600 Cubic Meters

| 5/10/64 | ALTITUDE
Tracy Barnes
Barnes 14-A balloons
Rosemount, Minnesota | U.S.A. | 11,780
Meters | (38,650 Feet) |
| 3/13/41 | DISTANCE
Boris Nevernov
URSS-VR 73 balloon
Dolgoprudny to Novosibirsk,
U.S.S.R. | U.S.S.R. | 2,766.814
KMS | (1,719.21 Miles) |

| 3/13/41 | DURATION
Boris Nevernov
URSS-VR 73 balloon
Dolgoprudny to Novosibirsk,
U.S.S.R. | U.S.S.R. | 69 Hours 20 Minutes | |

Sub-Class A-7
Between 1,600 and 2,000 Cubic Meters

5/10/64	ALTITUDE Tracy Barnes Barnes 14-A Balloon Rosemount, Minnesota	U.S.A.	11,780 Meters	(38,650 Feet)
3/13-16/41	DISTANCE Boris Nevernov URSS-VR 73 Balloon Dolgoprudny to Novosibirsk, USSR	U.S.S.R.	2.766.81 KMS	(1,719.21 Miles)
3/13-16/41	DURATION Boris Nevernov URSS-VR 73 Balloon Dolgoprudny to Novosibirsk, U.S.S.R.	U.S.S.R.	68 Hours 20 Minutes	

Sub-Class A-8
Between 2,200 and 3,000 Cubic Meters

5/10/64	ALTITUDE Tracy Barnes Barnes 14-A Balloon Rosemount, Minnesota	U.S.A.	11,780 Meters	(38,650 Feet)
10/5-10/76	DISTANCE Edward Yost Silver Fox GB-47 Milbridge, Maine to Lat. 37° 11' N Long. 20° 52' W	U.S.A.	3,983.18 KMS	(2,475.03 Miles)
10/5-10/76	DURATION Edward Yost Silver Fox GB-47 Milbridge, Maine to Lat. 37° 11' N Long. 20° 52' W	USA	107 Hours 37 Minutes	

Sub-Class A-9
Between 3,000 and 4,000 Cubic Meters

5/10/54	ALTITUDE Tracy Barnes Barnes 14-A Balloon Rosemount, Minnesota	U.S.A.	11,780 Meters	(38,650 Feet)
10/5-10/76	DISTANCE Edward Yost Silver Fox GB-47 Milbridge, Maine to Lat. 37° 11′ N Long. 20° 52′ W	U.S.A.	3,983.18 KMS	(2,475.03 Miles)
10/5-10/76	DURATION Edward Yost Silver Fox GB-47 Milbridge, Maine to Lat. 37° 11′ N Long. 20° 52′ W	U.S.A.	107 Hours 37 Minutes	

Sub-Class A-10
Over 4,000 Cubic Meters

5/4/61	ALTITUDE Cdr. Malcolm D. Ross USNR *Lee Lewis Memorial* Gulf of Mexico	U.S.A.	34,668 Meters	(113,739.9 Feet)
10/5-10/76	DISTANCE Edward Yost Silver Fox GB-47 Milbridge, Maine to Lat. 37ᶜ 11′ N Long. 20° 52′ W	U.S.A.	3,983.18 KMS	(2,475.03 Miles)
10/5-1/76	DURATION Edward Yost Silver Fox GB-47 Milbridge, Maine to Lat. 37° 11′ N Long. 20° 52′ W	U.S.A.	107 Hours 37 Minutes	

Sub-Class AA-11, AA-12, AA-13, AA-14, AA-15

| 8/12-17/78 | DISTANCE
Ben L. Abruzzo
Maxie L. Anderson
Cocommanders
Larry M. Newman,
Radio Operator
Double Eagle II
Presque Isle, Maine, U.S.A.
to Miserey, France | U.S.A. | 5001.22 KMS | (3,107.61 Miles) |

| 8/12-17/78 | DURATION
Ben L. Abruzzo
Maxie L. Anderson
Cocommanders
Double Eagle II
Presque Isle, Maine, U.S.A.
to Miserey, France | U.S.A. | 137 Hrs. 5 Min. 55 Sec. | |

HOT AIR BALLOONS

Sub-Class AX-1
Less Than 250 Cubic Meters

11/2/78	ALTITUDE Katherine E. Boland Boland Balloon Monarch Pass, Colorado	U.S.A.	3477 Meters	(11,407 Feet)
7/29/78	DISTANCE Katherine E. Boland Boland Balloon Farmington, Connecticut	U.S.A.	4.81 KMS	(2.99 Miles)
7/29/78	DURATION Katherine E. Boland Boland Balloon Farmington, Connecticut	U.S.A.	30 Minutes 5 Seconds	

Sub-Class AX-2
Between 250 and 400 Cubic Meters

11/2/78	ALTITUDE Katherine E. Boland Boland Balloon Monarch Pass, Colorado	U.S.A.	3477 Meters	(11,407 Feet)
3/13/75	DISTANCE Donna Wiederkehr Modified Raven hot air balloon St. Paul, Minnesota	U.S.A.	18.01 KMS	(11.19 Miles)
3/13/75	DURATION Donna Wiederkehr Modified Raven hot air balloon St. Paul, Minnesota	U.S.A.	2 Hours 40 Minutes	

Sub-Class AX-3
Between 400 and 600 Cubic Meters

| 11/1/78 | ALTITUDE
Brian Boland
Boland Balloon
Fairplay, Colorado | U.S.A. | 4642 Meters | (15,231 Feet) |

| 8/27/78 | DISTANCE
Brian Boland
Boland Balloon
Bridgeport, Connecticut/
Long Island Sound, New York | U.S.A. | 57.30 KMS | (35.60 Miles) |

| 8/27/78 | DURATION
Brian Boland
Boland Balloon
Bridgeport, Connecticut/
Long Island Sound, New York | U.S.A. | 3 Hours 46 Minutes | |

Sub-Class AX-4
Between 600 and 900 Cubic Meters

| 10/12/78 | ALTITUDE
Capt. Geoff Green
Cameron C-031
Northam, W.A. Australia | Hong
Kong | 6,941 Meters | (22,766.48 Feet) |

| 3/19/73 | DISTANCE
Matt H. Wiederkehr
Raven S40 Balloon
St. Paul, Minnesota | U.S.A. | 137.48 KMS | (85.43 Miles) |

| 3/19/73 | DURATION
Matt H. Wiederkehr
Raven S40 Balloon
St. Paul, Minnesota | U.S.A. | 5 Hrs. 5 Min. 55 Sec. | |

Sub-Class AX-5
Between 900 and 1,200 Cubic Meters

| 12/8/79 | ALTITUDE
Carol R. Davis
Firefly
Moriarty, New Mexico | U.S.A. | 9,540.24
Meters | (31,300 Feet) |

| 11/18/78 | DISTANCE
Simon Faithfull
Balloon Thunder
Münster-Eversen, West Germany | U.K. | 178 KMS | (110.6 Miles) |

| 3/19/73 | DURATION
Matt H. Wiederkehr
Raven S40 Balloon
St. Paul, Minnesota | U.S.A. | 5 Hrs. 5 Min. 55 Sec. | |

Sub-Class AX-6
Between 1,200 and 1,600 Cubic Meters

| 8/26/77 | ALTITUDE
G. Green
Cameron O-56
Northam, Australia | U.K. | 9,296.4
Meters | (30,492.19 Ft.) |

| 3/23/74 | DISTANCE
Denise Wiederkehr
Raven S50A Balloon
St. Paul, Minn., to
Waupun, Wisc. | U.S.A. | 369.99 KMS | (288.04 Miles) |

| 4/17/78 | DURATION
Julian R. P. Nott
Thunder 56A
Pitch and Green–Barrow
Haven, New Holland | U.K. | 11 Hours 20 Minutes | |

Sub-Class AX-7
Between 1,600 and 2,200 Cubic Meters

| 6/10/76 | ALTITUDE
Julian R. P. Mott
Thunder
Kurman, Republic of South Africa | U.K. | 11,286
Meters | (37,027.5 Feet) |

| 1/25/78 | DISTANCE
Philip Clark
Cameron *Sungas*
Bristol, U.K. | U.K. | 564.47 KMS | (350.74 Miles) |

| 3/7/74 | DURATION
Matt H. Wiederkehr
Raven S55A Balloon
St. Paul, Minn., to Butte, Neb. | U.S.A. | 16 Hours 16 Minutes | |

Sub-Class AX-8
Between 2,200 and 3,000 Cubic Meters

| 9/27/75 | ALTITUDE
Kingswood Sprott, Jr.
Raven S60A Balloon
Lakeland, Florida | U.S.A. | 11,822.91
Meters | (38,789 Feet) |

1/25/78	DISTANCE	U.K.	564.47 KMS	(350.74 Miles)
	Philip Clark			
	Cameron *Sungas*			
	Bristol, U.K.			
3/7/74	DURATION	U.S.A.	16 Hours 16 Minutes	
	Matt H. Wiederkehr			
	Raven S55A Balloon			
	St. Paul, Minnesota, to			
	Butte, Neb.			

Sub-Class AX-9
Between 3,000 and 4,000 Cubic Meters

8/1/79	ALTITUDE	U.S.A.	16,154.4 Meters	(53,000 Feet)*
	Chauncey M. Dunn			
	Raven S-66-A Balloon			
	N-5682-C			
	Indianola, Iowa			
1/25/78	DISTANCE	U.K.	564.47 KMS	(350.74 Miles)
	Philip Clark			
	Cameron *Sungas*			
	Bristol, U.K.			
3/7/74	DURATION	U.S.A.	16 Hours 16 Minutes	
	Matt H. Wiederkehr			
	Raven S55A Balloon			
	St. Paul, Minnesota,			
	to Butte, Nebraska			

Sub-Class AX-10, AX-11, AX-12, AX-13, AX-14, AX-15
Over 4,000 Cubic Meters

8/1/79	ALTITUDE	U.S.A.	16,154.4 Meters	(53,000 Feet)*
	Chauncey M. Dunn			
	Raven S-66-A Balloon N-5682-C			
	Indianola, Iowa			
1/25/78	DISTANCE	U.K.	564.47 KMS	(350.74 Miles)
	Philip Clark			
	Cameron *Sungas*			
	Bristol, U.K.			
11/21/75	DURATION	U.S.A.	24 Hours 8 Minutes	
	Van Alstine, Comstock			

*On Oct. 31, 1980, Julian Nott of Great Britain broke this record with an ascent of 55,900 feet in Longmont, Colorado. As of this writing, the NAA had not yet made the record official.

CLASS "AM" – BALLOONS

Sub-Class AM-10
Between 4,000 and 6,000 Cubic Meters

7/26-30/78	DISTANCE Donald Cameron Christopher Davey Balloon Cameron St. Johns, Newfoundland, Bay of Biscay	U.K.	3,339.086 KMS	(2,074.81 Miles)
7/26-30/78	DURATION Donald Cameron Christopher Davey Balloon Cameron St. Johns, Newfoundland, Bay of Biscay	U.K.	96 Hours 24 Minutes	

Sub-Class AM-11
Between 6,000 and 9,000 Cubic Meters

7/26-30/78	DISTANCE Donald Cameron Christopher Davey Balloon Cameron St. Johns, Newfoundland, Bay of Biscaý	U.K.	3,339.086 KMS	(2,074.81 Miles)
7/26-30/78	DURATION Donald Cameron Christopher Davey Balloon Cameron St. Johns, Newfoundland, Bay of Biscay	U.K.	96 Hours 24 Minutes	

Sub-Class AM-12
Between 9,000 and 12,000 Cubic Meters

7/26-30/78	DISTANCE Donald Cameron Christopher Davey Balloon Cameron St. Johns, Newfoundland, Bay of Biscay	U.K.	3,339.086 KMS	(2,074.81 Miles)
7/26-30/78	DURATION Donald Cameron Christopher Davey Balloon Cameron St. Johns, Newfoundland, Bay of Biscay	U.K.	96 Hours 24 Minutes	

Sub-Class AM-13
Between 12,000 and 16,000 Cubic Meters

7/26-30/78	DISTANCE Donald Cameron Christopher Davey Balloon Cameron St. Johns, Newfoundland, Bay of Biscay	U.K.	3,339.086 KMS	(2,074.81 Miles)
7/26-30/78	DURATION Donald Cameron Christopher Davey Balloon Cameron St. Johns, Newfoundland, Bay of Biscay	U.K.	96 Hours 24 Minutes	

Sub-Class AM-14
Between 16,000 and 22,000 Cubic Meters

7/26	DISTANCE Donald Cameron Christopher Davey Balloon Cameron St. Johns, Newfoundland, Bay of Biscay	U.K.	3,339.086 KMS	(2,074.81 Miles)
7/26-30/78	DURATION Donald Cameron Christopher Davey Balloon Cameron St. Johns, Newfoundland, Bay of Biscay	U.K.	96 Hours 24 Minutes	

Sub-Class AM-15
Between 22,000 Cubic Meters and above

7/26-30/78	DISTANCE Donald Cameron Christopher Davey Balloon Cameron St. Johns, Newfoundland, Bay of Biscay	U.K.	3,339.086 KMS	(2,074.81 Miles)
7/26-30/78	DURATION Donald Cameron Christopher Davey Balloon Cameron St. Johns, Newfoundland, Bay of Biscay	U.K.	96 Hours 24 Minutes	

Glossary of Ballooning Terms

A	An absolute designation by the FAI for the category of gas balloon.
Abort	Discontinue a takeoff or a flight.
Acrophobia	The fear of being at a great height above the ground.
Aeronate	Early term for a tethered or captive balloon.
Aeronaut	Balloon pilot or passenger.
Aerostat	Any lighter-than-air craft kept in flight solely by aerostatic forces and without any direct means of horizontal propulsion.
Aerostation	The art (and science) of operating lighter-than-air vehicles.
AGL	Above ground level, an altitude term used to indicate height of the balloon above the actual ground.
Airport traffic area	A cylinder of airspace 5 miles in radius and 3,000 feet deep over any airport with an operating control tower.
Airspeed	The speed with which an aircraft moves through the air. A free balloon propelled by the movement of the surrounding air always flies at zero airspeed.
Airway	An air corridor designated by the Federal Aviation Administration (FAA), controlled by Air Traffic Control (ATC) and marked by radio navigational beacons.
Airworthiness certificate	A certificate issued by the FAA based on an inspection by a licensed inspector.
Altimeter	An aneroid barometer that indicates the altitude of an aircraft above sea level by measuring air pressure and reading out the result in feet above sea level.
Altitude	Height in feet above mean sea level. Also given as height above the ground over which an aircraft is flying.
Anemometer	An instrument which reads and records wind velocity.
Annual inspection	An inspection that must be completed every twelve months to verify the condition of airworthiness of a flying machine.

Apex	The uppermost point or crown of the balloon envelope, where the ends of gores and load tapes come together; the north pole.
Apex rope	The rope attached to the apex of the balloon, used by the ground crew during inflation to control the movement of the balloon. Also called apex or crown line.
Appendix	The sleeve at the bottom or on the side of a gas balloon, through which the balloon is filled and through which expanding gas may escape.
Approach	The final stage in flight during which a flying machine transitions from an aerial to a ground environment. The approach precedes the actual landing and is used to make sure the landing is effective.
Ascension	The process of rising from the ground to some level in the atmosphere or climbing to a higher altitude by adding heat to the envelope or, in gas ballooning, casting off ballast.
ATC	Air Traffic Control, a function of the FAA.
Attitude	Describes a vehicle's position relative to the horizon.
Aviation charts	Charts used in all types of aviation.
Aviation radios	Radios designed to transmit or receive on the frequency bands used in aviation, primarily the VHF frequencies between 108.0 and 135.95 MHz.
AX	A designation by the FAI referring to the category of hot air balloon.
Ballast	Disposable weight—usually sand—used and carried in gas-type balloons to assist in maintaining a regular flight altitude and for checking descents.
Balloon	A lighter-than-air vehicle that derives its lift from either a specific gas—such as hydrogen, helium, or methane (coal gas)—or hot air. Used also to describe the envelope, a bag of tightly woven, strong material with a good resistance to heat and a minimum porosity—in the case of hot air balloons. In gas balloons, usually of a high-grade plastic such as Du Pont Mylar.
Balloonmeister	A person who has the authority and responsibility to exercise operational control of all ground-based balloon activities.
Barograph	A barometer, usually aneroid, that automatically records variations in atmospheric pressure—often as altitude or height above a mean point—on a revolving paper-covered cylinder.

Basket

The carrying part of the balloon vehicle, in which burner, controls, instruments, fuel, and aeronauts are contained. Also called *gondola.*

Blast

The violent outburst and sound of expanding gas when propane is burned by the airborne heaters of a hot air balloon.

Blast off

High-speed lift-off using positive buoyancy, used typically when there is a breeze and the aeronaut needs to make a speed ascent. See also *weigh off.*

Blast valve

A high-pressure fuel valve operated either fully open or fully closed.

Blimp

A nonrigid or semirigid airship.

Btu

British thermal unit, a designation used internationally to measure the amount of heat.

Buoyancy

The tendency of a balloon to rise or float in air.

Burner

A unit carried in the gondola of hot air balloons, to burn propane gas to heat the air in the envelope.

Captive balloon

A balloon restrained to the ground by a mooring or tether line.

CB radio

Citizens-band radio, used in ballooning to facilitate communication between the balloon and the ground crew.

Ceiling

The distance between the ground and a broken or overcast cloud cover.

Chase crew

The ground crew members who, after assisting with the inflation and launch, follow the balloon in a chase vehicle to retrieve it after landing.

Checklist

An itemized list of procedures and the best way to ensure that you are operating your balloon correctly.

Commercial pilot

A pilot certified to fly persons or freight for hire. In ballooning, a commercially rated pilot may also give flight instruction.

Compass

The magnetic compass, which always points to magnetic north. A compass is optional equipment on hot air balloons and required on every other type of aircraft except hang-gliders.

Cross-country

Any flight covering a distance of more than 25 nautical miles.

Crown line

A handling line approximately 100 feet long attached to the apex or crown of the balloon and used to hold the balloon steady during inflation and deflation.

Cruise valve	An adjustable valve which controls the flow of fuel through the burner. Also called *metering valve*.
Deflation port	The rip panel or section of the upper envelope that separates to allow hot air to escape, thereby deflating the balloon.
Dirigible	A lighter-than-air craft equipped with a power source and means of directional control.
Drag line	A long, usually heavy rope that is dangled from the gondola of gas balloons to help regulate altitude during low-level flight by acting as regulating ballast. Not usually found in hot air balloons.
Drift	A movement away from a *selected* flight path, caused by the wind. The term is sometimes used when the wind doesn't behave as forecast, and your balloon "drifts" from the tentative course you had plotted on your chart.
Envelope	The fabric part of a balloon, which contains either gas or hot air. It is made of gores of specially woven and proof-stressed synthetic material.
Envelope bag	The bag into which the envelope is stuffed for the purpose of ground transportation.
Equator	The horizontal line at which the diameter of the balloon is greatest.
Equilibrium	The stage at which the lifting capability of the balloon equals the force of gravity, keeping it at a constant altitude.
FAA	Federal Aviation Administration; can be found in local phone books under U.S. Government, Department of Transportation.
False lift	The venturi effect of the wind that could cause the balloon to lift off before true equilibrium is reached.
FAR	Federal Aviation Regulations.
Forced landing	Landing because you have no other options—such as when you've run out of fuel.
FPM	Feet per minute.
Free balloon	A balloon that is not tethered to the ground in any way.
FSS	Flight-service station, an ATC facility maintained by the FAA to offer services to pilots, used by balloonists primarily for preflight weather briefings.

Gondola	Basket
Gore	A lengthy piece of balloon fabric which tapers at each end to form sections of a spherical or other shaped envelope when sewn to other gores.
Gross weight	The weight of the balloon, gondola, equipment, fuel, pilot, and passengers. There *is* a maximum allowable gross weight, but the general term is for the total weight at any given time.
Ground crew	The ground-based crew needed to assist in inflating, landing, and deflating the balloon.
Ground handling ropes	Various ropes attached to the envelope and used by the ground crew to control the movement of the balloon during inflation.
Ground inflator, blower, also cold inflator, blower	A gasoline- or electric-powered fan, usually a cage-type blower, used for preliminary ground inflation instead of flapping the envelope full of cold air—which takes much longer.
Ground speed	The speed of a flying machine in relation to the ground over which it is flying. Ground speed relates to distance traveled over the ground. Air speed relates to speed relative to the air through which the aircraft is flying. A hot air or free balloon only has ground speed, since it travels with the wind. A blimp or rigid airship which is powered has both ground and air speed.
Helium	A nonflammable lighter-than-air gas.
Hydrogen	A flammable lighter-than-air gas.
Inflation	The process by which air is forced into the balloon envelope and heated to provide lift.
Kitchen gas	A natural gas used occasionally in gas balloons. It is flammable and less efficient than hydrogen or helium, but cheaper than either.
Knot	A unit of wind speed in nautical miles per hour, where one nautical miles equals 6,076 feet.
Landing site	An obstruction-free site selected by the pilot appropriate for landing the balloon.
Launch site	An obstruction-free site selected for launch.
Lift	The amount of lifting action produced by gas or hot air in lighter-than-air craft, or by the combination of airfoil and speed in heavier-than-air craft.

Load ring

The point of attachment of suspension lines and rigging beneath the mouth of the balloon.

Load tape

A flat vertical or horizontal stress-bearing webbed nylon member used in the construction of hot air balloon envelopes.

Log book

A book in which to keep a record of pilot and aircraft flight time.

LPG

Liquefied petroleum gas; propane, is one example.

LTA

Lighter-than-air craft.

Maneuvering vent

A vent which can be opened or closed by the pilot during flight in order to reduce the lift temporarily.

Metering valve

A high-pressure fuel valve that is used to regulate propane flow with precision.

Mouth

The large opening at the base of the hot air balloon.

MPH

Speed measured in statute miles per hour.

MSL

Altitude above mean sea level.

Nautical mile

A distance equaling 1.15 statute miles.

Panel

A fabric section sewn as part of a gore in a balloon envelope.

Pilot light

A separate small propane-fueled burner with a constant flame for the purpose of igniting the main burner.

Propane

A clean-burning liquefied petroleum gas or a heavy flammable gaseous hydrocarbon fuel.

Pyrometer

The instrument which displays the information from a thermocouple used to measure the temperature of the hot air in the upper section of a hot air balloon.

Ratings

Designations issued by the FAA stating pilot qualifications.

Redline temperature

The maximum safe temperature beyond which heat may damage envelope fabric.

Rip line

A line from the ripping panel, or deflation port, which leads to the gondola, usually made of bright red fabric as a visual warning that it is not to be used except when needed. A tug of the rip line opens the deflation port, permitting the hot air to escape.

SIGMET	*Sig*nificant *Met*eorological advisory, usually warning of impending hazardous weather conditions.
Sink	Rate of descent.
Skirt	A section of material beneath the throat to protect the area around the burner once inflation is completed, installed on some hot air balloons to reduce loss of burner heat by gusts of wind across the throat.
Solo flight	A flight in which the pilot is the only person on board.
Sparker	A device for igniting the pilot light.
Stratosphere	The coldest region of the atmosphere, generally from about 35,000 to 80,000 feet.
Superstructure	A metallic or wooden structure constructed as a vertical extension above the basket of a balloon.
Suspension cables	The stainless steel wires designed to transmit loads from the basket superstructure or burner frame assembly to the envelope load tapes.
Telltale	Special heat-sensitive material placed within the top of a hot air balloon to provide warning when temperatures have developed that might cause damage to the envelope material.
Tether line	An anchor line used during training or for a captive balloon flight, in no- or low-wind conditions.
Thermal	A rising column of warm spiraling air.
Throat	The area near the mouth or base of the envelope.
Trajectory	The flight path traced out by a balloon.
Transceiver	A radio which receives and transmits.
Transponder	An electronic pulse instrument which automatically responds to interrogation by ground-based radar, permitting ATC to determine accurately the position of an aircraft.
Valves	The special-purpose valves of a propane-burner system, including the blast valve, meter valve, pilot-light valve, pressure-relief valve, and vapor-bleed valve.
Variometer	An electrically powered flight instrument designed to tell vertical air speed or the rate of climb or descent.

Velocity

Speed of movement, usually applied to winds.

Visibility

The greatest distance at which landmarks can be seen by the unaided eye.

Weigh off

The process of bringing a balloon into neutral equilibrium so that it neither rises nor settles. In hot air balloons this is done by adjusting heat; in gas balloons by adding or removing ballast.

Winds aloft

The winds at given altitudes, usually higher than surface winds.

Index